1 Corinthians

1 Corinthians

WESLEY R. WILLIS

VICTOR BOOKS
A DIVISION OF SCRIPTURE PRESS PUBLICATIONS INC.
USA CANADA ENGLAND

Unless otherwise noted, Scripture quotations in this
Bible study are from the *Holy Bible, New International
Version*, © 1973, 1978, 1984, International Bible Society. Used by permission of Zondervan Bible Publishers.

Recommended Dewey Decimal Classification: 227.2
Suggested Subject Heading: BIBLE, N.T.–EPISTLES

Library of Congress Catalog Card Number: 88-62863
ISBN: 0-89693-649-X

© 1989 by SP Publications, Inc. All rights reserved.
Printed in the United States of America. No part of this
book may be reproduced without written permission,
except for brief quotations in books, critical articles, and
reviews.

VICTOR BOOKS
A division of SP Publications, Inc.
        Wheaton, Illinois 60187

CONTENTS

How to Use This Study   7
Introduction to the First Epistle to the Corinthians   9

1. **1 CORINTHIANS 1:1–2:16** *What It Means to Be Different*   13

2. **1 CORINTHIANS 3:1–4:21** *How Christians Ought to Act*   21

3. **1 CORINTHIANS 5:1–6:20** *Confronting Sin among Believers*   29

4. **1 CORINTHIANS 7:1-40** *Christian Marriage Guidelines*   35

5. **1 CORINTHIANS 8:1–9:27** *Christian Rights and Obligations*   42

6. **1 CORINTHIANS 10:1–11:1** *When Christians Disagree*   49

7. **1 CORINTHIANS 11:2-34** *Celebrating Jesus' Sacrifice*   55

8. **1 CORINTHIANS 12:1-31** *Believers Equipped for Service*   61

9. **1 CORINTHIANS 13:1-13** *The Most Excellent Way*   68

10. **1 CORINTHIANS 14:1-40** *Nurturing a Well-balanced Church*   74

11. **1 CORINTHIANS 15:1-34** *Believers Assured of Resurrection*   82

12. **1 CORINTHIANS 15:35–16:24** *Christians in the Future and the Present*   88

How to Use This Study

Personal Growth Bible Studies are designed to help you understand God's Word and how it applies to everyday life. To complete the studies in this book, you will need to use a Bible. A good modern translation of the Bible, such as the *New International Version* or the *New American Standard Bible*, will give you the most help. (NOTE: the questions in this book are based on the *New International Version*.)

You will find it helpful to follow a similar sequence with each study. First, read the introductory paragraphs. This material helps set the tone and lay the groundwork for the passage to be studied. Once you have completed this part of the study, spend time reading the assigned passage in your Bible. This will give you a general feel for the content of the passage.

Having completed the preliminaries, you are then ready to dig deeper into the Scripture passage. Each study is divided into several sections so that you can take a close-up look at the smaller parts of the larger passage. These sections each begin with a synopsis of the Scripture to be studied in that section. Following each synopsis is a two-part study section made up of *Explaining the Text* and *Examining the Text*.

Explaining the Text gives background notes and commentary to help you understand points in the text that may not be readily apparent. After reading any comments that appear in *Explaining the Text*, answer each question under *Examining the Text*.

At the end of each study is a section called *Experiencing the Text*. The questions in this section focus on the application of biblical principles to life. You may find that some of the questions can be answered immediately; others will require that you spend more time reflecting on the passages you have just studied.

The distinctive format of the Personal Growth Bible Studies makes them easy to use individually as well as for group study. If the majority of those in your group answer the questions before the group meeting, spend most of your time together discussing the *Experiencing* questions.

If, on the other hand, members have not answered the questions ahead of time and you have adequate time in your group meeting, work through all of the questions together.

However you use this series of studies, our prayer is that you will understand the Bible as never before, and that because of this understanding, you will experience a rich and dynamic Christian life. If questions of interpretation arise in the course of this study, we recommend you refer to the two-volume set, *The Bible Knowledge Commentary*, edited by John F. Walvoord and Roy B. Zuck (Victor Books, 1984, 1986).

Introduction to the First Epistle to the Corinthians

Some years ago a biography was written about a man who had the vision for ministering in the heart of New Orleans. He was described as the Chaplain of Bourbon Street. This is the street in New Orleans that draws people from across the country for drinking, risqué shows, and all sorts of immorality and debauchery. On most nights, and well into the early morning hours, the streets rock with the raucous laughter of revelers accompanied by the live music of Dixieland jazz bands.

In this context, a chaplain seems to be an incredible paradox. And yet God gave this man a vision to minister to those so obviously in need, who were being ignored by most Christians. Both performer and patron—every bartender, dancer, female impersonator, prostitute, and homosexual—desperately needed to hear the Gospel of Christ. And in this context, the Chaplain of Bourbon Street ministered.

The church at Corinth existed in a far worse context than Bourbon Street. Just as the Chaplain of Bourbon Street served God in the midst of prevalent sin, so the Corinthian Christians were light in the midst of darkness. The city was known particularly for its sexual looseness. Every form of evil perversion was available. And not only available, but openly flaunted, often in the name of religion. The temple of the Greek goddess Aphrodite, goddess of love and beauty, was the focus of Corinthian religion. Every evening a thousand temple prostitutes would seduce the men of Corinth, all in the name of worship.

Corinth was a trade center for both sea and land commerce. It was the meeting place of East and West. It was a place where virtually anything was available for a price. And often the charge was exacted in the form of human suffering and degradation.

As nearly as we can tell, the Apostle Paul visited Corinth three times. His first stay lasted about eighteen months, during which he led a number of Corinthians to place their faith in Christ and helped them to establish a church (see Acts 18). His second visit occurred between the writing of 1 and 2 Corinthians, and he probably visited again after writing 2 Corinthians.

As you can well imagine, the new believers who turned to Christ out of the context of the city of Corinth had much to learn about the true God and His expectations. The Book of 1 Corinthians addresses many of these struggles. The first six chapters include teaching about specific sins, factionalism, and rivalry within the church. Chapter 7 begins the section where Paul answers questions brought to him by members of the house of Chloe.

In the midst of his answers to questions about marriage and remarriage, Christian living, spiritual gifts, and church behavior, Paul inserted a poetic masterpiece extolling the virtues of love (chapter 13). Certainly this is the most beautiful love poem ever written because it describes perfect love—the love of God. And this model of love has been given to us as the standard by which we should live. Paul concluded the book with a brief exposition of the end times and what the Resurrection of Christ means to us.

We pray that as you study through this intensely relevant book, the Holy Spirit will teach you through it. May your spiritual life be enriched, and may you grow and mature through this time. We pray that you will finish this study looking forward to the return of Christ with keen anticipation.

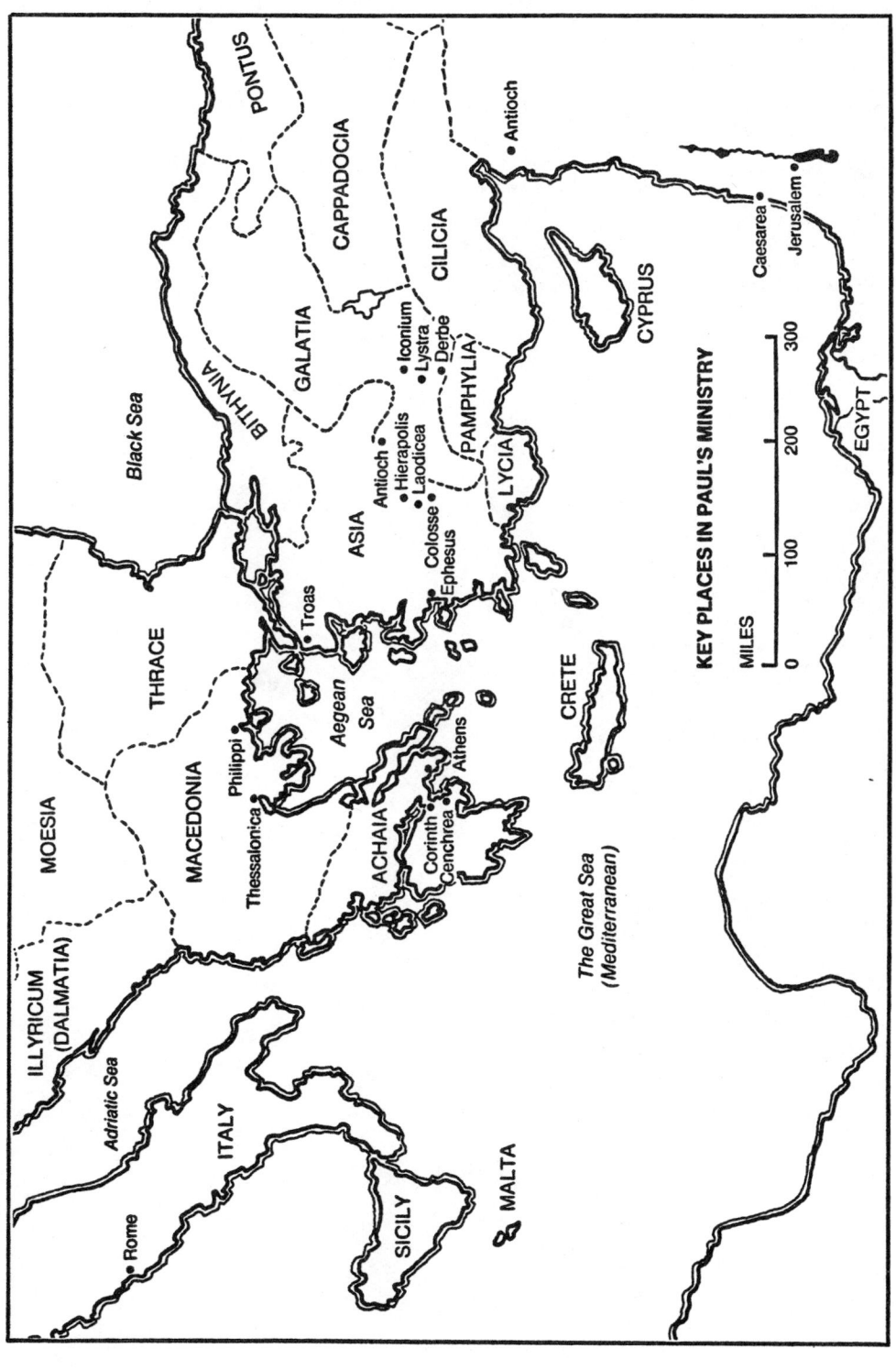

STUDY ONE

1 Corinthians 1:1–2:16

What It Means to Be Different

Recently I was in an airport waiting for a flight and decided to pass the time by observing people going by. I rarely fly on a Sunday morning, but this trip was an exception, which was fortunate for me since this is a prime time to pursue the sport of people-watching. It's boring during the week (when I usually fly) because about eighty percent of the travelers are businesspeople. Most of them look as if they have been stamped out with the same cookie cutter—a parade of blue suits neatly wrapped around white shirts and maroon ties.

But Sunday morning is when vacationers and students fly. All around me I saw families. One father dashed off regularly to retrieve a "terrible two" just before he darted out of the terminal or was "conveyed" to a baggage compartment bound for Singapore.

But the most fascinating part was observing the garb of many of the travelers—especially the young women. Bizarre outfits with huge floppy sweatshirts in gaudy colors, many emblazoned with inscrutable mottoes. Faded jeans, that obviously had never seen a lick of work, tucked into bulky-knit socks designed for hiking the Appalachian Trail.

But the really curious feature was that, in one sense, they all looked alike. Bizarre? Yes. Gaudy? Unquestionably. But they obviously had taken great care to be unique "like everyone else." I couldn't help but think how very human that tendency is. We try so hard to be individuals, but we don't want to appear too different. This carries over into the way we think also. And it's not new to our era. Paul encountered such attitudes among the Corinthians. They wanted to follow Christ but also they were reluctant to vary too much from their culture. And so the Corinthian believers carried many of the attitudes and actions of contemporary Corinth into their church, just as we are prone to do today. The Corinthians needed to understand Paul's message, but we do too. Let's dare to stand out from the crowd—to be different for Christ.

A. INTRODUCTION *(1 Cor. 1:1-9)*. When we must bring up an unpleasant topic of conversation with another person, often we begin by expressing something that is good. Even though Paul had to correct grievous faults in the Corinthian church, he was able to begin with positive, encouraging words. He recognized their good points and commended the Corinthians for them.

Examining the Text	*Explaining the Text*
1. Read 1 Corinthians 1:1-9. Who were the authors of this epistle? (v. 1)	1. Sosthenes (SAHS-thin-ees) apparently was the one who wrote down this letter as Paul dictated it. The technical word used to describe a person who serves in this role is "amanuensis."
2. Who (in addition to the Corinthians) were the recipients of this letter? (v. 2)	
3. What can we understand about the believers in Corinth from these introductory comments that Paul made? (vv. 2, 5, 7, 9) Based on these observations, what kind of a church would you expect the Corinthian church to be?	3. "Sanctified" (v. 2) does not imply that they were living holy lives. It means "set apart" to God. Often this is called positional holiness because a believer's position before God is holy, based on the finished work of Christ. However, beyond position, believers also ought to be growing in practical holiness as they are maturing spiritually.
4. Why was Paul thankful for the Corinthian believers? (v. 4) What did Paul expect God to do for the Corinthians? (v. 8)	4. Although Paul was thankful for the believers in Corinth, it was not because they had no problems or were already fully mature. Actually they struggled with major problems, and most of the rest of this epistle addresses those problems.

What It Means to Be Different

Explaining the Text	*Examining the Text*
	5. What was the reason that Paul could have strong expectations for the Corinthians? (v. 9)

B. PROBLEMS IN THE CHURCH *(1 Cor. 1:10-17).* If the Corinthians were waiting for the "second shoe to drop," they didn't have long to wait. Immediately after commending them for those positive characteristics, Paul addressed some of the major problems in the church. This section deals with rivalry and factionalism.

Explaining the Text	*Examining the Text*
1. When believers relate properly to each other, there is a twofold benefit. Certain things will not happen, and other things will occur. Here Paul considers both aspects.	1. Read 1 Corinthians 1:10-17. According to verse 10, what did Paul plead with the believers in the church at Corinth to do? What did Paul indicate would be the results (both positive and negative)?
2. Paul (the Apostle to the Gentiles), Apollos (who apparently was a golden-tongued orator), and Cephas (the Apostle Peter) each had ministered to all or to some of the Corinthians. And for this reason, the Corinthians gravitated toward their favorites, setting up a false rivalry.	2. What seems to be the reason that there was significant conflict among the believers? (vv. 11-12) How do we see the same dynamics at work in various churches today?

Examining the Text	*Explaining the Text*
3. What rationale did Paul present to show how inappropriate it was to have divisions based on personal favorites among Christians? (v. 13)	3. There seemed to be almost a political rivalry among the Corinthian Christians as they chose up sides, and then argued for their personal favorites.
4. How could the fact that Paul baptized very few new converts in Corinth help to defuse the contrived rivalry? (vv. 14-16)	
5. What was Paul's mission in life? (v. 17) What did he not depend on to fulfill that mission?	5. Paul did not intend to demean baptism, but he did want to emphasize that Christ was the focus of his ministry. Paul was not concerned with building followers or personal disciples for himself.
6. What could have been the outcome if Paul had emphasized human wisdom instead of the message of the cross? (v. 17)	

C. GENUINE AND FALSE WISDOM CONTRASTED *(1 Cor. 1:18–2:5)*. Just because someone is wise in one area of life does not mean that person understands other areas. There are many who may be wealthy or wise according to the world's evaluation, but who are hopelessly ignorant when it comes to spiritual understanding.

Examining the Text	*Explaining the Text*
1. Read 1 Corinthians 1:18–2:5. What are two responses to the message of the cross? (vv. 18-19)	1. In this section Paul contrasted preaching of the Gospel with "wisdom," which he condemned. He was not speaking of true

What It Means to Be Different   17

Explaining the Text

wisdom but of a psuedo-wisdom ("philosophies of this age," "wisdom of the world," v. 20). These were popularly accepted as wisdom, but in reality had nothing to do with true wisdom.

Examining the Text

What determines whether a person will respond to preaching as "foolishness" or as "the power of God"?

2. What current illustration can you cite that demonstrates how the message of the cross still is in conflict with "worldly wisdom"?

3. Throughout this section, Paul used the words "wisdom" and "philosophy" with a tongue-in-cheek definition. This is because they were not true wisdom or philosophy, but weak human substitutes.

3. If human wisdom is inadequate, how do people comprehend the truth about God? (v. 21)

4. Both of the groups whom Paul described illustrate responses to the message of Jesus Christ. Perhaps it seemed too ordinary, or too simple, for the Jews and the Greeks to accept. And even today, there are those who want to complicate the message of the Gospel. But the Bible teaches that all humans are sinners, alienated from God. And we can be saved only through accepting the free gift of salvation, purchased by Jesus with His sacrificial death on the cross.

4. What were the Jews and the Greeks seeking? (v. 22)

How did they respond to the preaching of the cross? (v. 23)

In contrast, how did those who accepted Paul's message respond to the preaching of the cross? (vv. 24-25)

And how do you respond?

Examining the Text	Explaining the Text
5. Why do you think that God chose the things and the people that He did to proclaim the truth of the Gospel? (vv. 26-31)	5. It is important to recognize that Paul did not demean true wisdom or nobility. However, these alone will never bring a person salvation or confer status in God's eyes.
6. How did Paul approach the Corinthians with his message? (vv. 1-3) Why did he choose to come this way? (v. 4) And what was the result? (v. 5)	6. Paul seemed to work aggressively at not giving even the slightest hint that he was accommodating his message, or his presentation of that message, to preconceived notions or the prejudices of his hearers.

D. TRUE SPIRITUAL WISDOM *(1 Cor. 2:6-16)*. Everybody loves to be let in on a secret. But the problem with most real secrets is that you cannot tell them to anyone else. However, the most exciting secret in the world was designed to be revealed to everyone. This secret is the truth, revealed through Christ, of how God provided for us to be reconciled to Him.

Examining the Text	Explaining the Text
1. Read 1 Corinthians 2:6-16. How does Paul's use of wisdom here differ with how he used it in the previous section? (v. 6)	1. The words "mature" and "secret" indicate that the wisdom Paul referred to here is different from the human or earthly wisdom referred to previously.
2. What is the source of the wisdom of God, and when did it originate? (v. 7)	

What It Means to Be Different

Explaining the Text

3. The quote (v. 9) comes from Isaiah 64:4 and contrasts what the human mind can conceive with the magnitude of what God has planned for those who love Him.

4. A very wise person, who tries to understand spiritual truth without the insight of God's Spirit, remains blind to that truth. Such a person is ignorant of spiritual truth and cannot perceive it.

5. When persons are born again, they receive the Spirit of God. This puts them in tune with spiritual truth and enables them to comprehend reality.

Examining the Text

3. How did people demonstrate that they did not understand the true wisdom from God? (v. 8)

4. What are the two spirits that Paul referred to in verses 10-13?

What is the difference in the results of these two spirits? (v. 14)

5. How does the person without the Spirit of God respond to spiritual truth? (v. 14)

How does the person with the Spirit of God respond to spiritual truth? (vv. 15-16)

And how do you respond to spiritual truth?

Experiencing the Text

1. Even though we who are Christians have been sanctified positionally, we also should see progress in holiness in our daily lives. Take a moment and evaluate your life. Do you see growth in holy living? What examples of such growth can you cite?

2. What examples of party rivalry can you cite among Christians today?

Describe how Christians can fall into such a trap, and what can be done to avoid party rivalry.

3. How could your education or money get in the way of your response to Christ?

What can you do to keep this from happening?

4. Describe people who have rejected spiritual truth and, although they may be very wise, are spiritually ignorant.

How has your response to spiritual truth affected your life?

STUDY TWO

1 Corinthians 3:1–4:21

How Christians Ought to Act

Some years ago, when our sons were younger, I arrived home one day to find two of them "going at each other" in the garage. One of them served a newspaper route at the time, and the other had volunteered to help him.

As I entered the garage, I heard one of our sons tell the other, "You are so stupid!" The other immediately shot back, "Don't be such a jerk!" Since to me that didn't sound like edifying communication, I decided that it was time to enter the conversation.

"Boys, boys," I said, "do you know what you sound like?" One of them looked up at me with a scowl on his face and replied in a disgusted tone, "Yeah, brothers!" Unfortunately, at that moment I lost my composure and began laughing at the entire situation, including the reply. And when I started laughing, they both responded similarly—especially the one who had come up with the "bright reply."

I'm not sure how effective my subsequent lecture was, but at least my response defused the situation. Later I began thinking about the dynamics of the situation. We recognized the humor because we knew that our son's reply was all too accurate. Far too often brothers demonstrate the ability to draw out the worst from each other. Fortunately, the tendency seems to decrease as they grow older. In fact, they even seem to be turning into good friends—some of the time.

Since brothers are members of the same family, and since they share so many common experiences, it seems that they ought to be very good friends. But sometimes rivalry and competition take over. And then there is conflict. How similar is our experience in the body of Christ. We have so much in common with fellow Christians, but sometimes competition and rivalry eclipse what we share. And then hostility and argument arise. Paul recognized just such circumstances in the Corinthian church. Even though they had much in common, they also had great conflict. And Paul wrote to encourage them to resolve their problems.

A. RIVALRY IN THE CHURCH *(1 Cor. 3:1-9)*. Even though the Corinthians had received the basic message of the Gospel, they failed to comprehend many of its implications. And just as children often do, the Corinthians nurtured petty rivalry and competition among those who should have been cooperating.

Examining the Text	*Explaining the Text*
1. Read 1 Corinthians 3:1-9. How did Paul view the spiritual maturity of the Corinthian believers? (v. 1)	1. It is possible (as in the case of the Corinthians) that a person can be born again and yet still be very immature spiritually (an infant).
2. What kind of message or truth do you think Paul referred to when he described what the Corinthians needed as "milk," not "meat"? (v. 2)	2. A fuller discussion of maturity and spiritual "milk" and "meat" can be found in Hebrews 5:11–6:3.
3. What were two specific indications that believers in Corinth were acting and responding on the basis of worldly rather than spiritual wisdom? (v. 3)	
4. What was the underlying error of the worldly rivalry and petty bickering at Corinth? (vv. 3-4)	4. It is important to recognize that the various ministers to Corinth (Paul, Apollos, and Cephas) all received their mandates from the Lord, and He alone should receive glory.
5. What ought to characterize proper relationships between various ministers of the Gospel? (vv. 5-8)	5. It is very clear that no one minister of the Gospel has a corner on the ministry. And while God has given great gifts to His servants, this is not an occasion for boasting or for generating a sense of competition.

How Christians Ought to Act

Explaining the Text	*Examining the Text*
	6. What metaphors (word pictures) did Paul use to describe the church—the body of Christ? (v. 9)
	How are these descriptive of what a local church ought to be?
	How well do they describe your church?

B. COOPERATION IN THE CHURCH *(1 Cor. 3:10-23)*. Obviously, no building can be any better than the foundation on which it is built. And yet it can be far worse. A very strong foundation may have a superstructure that is worthless. Paul was concerned that both the foundation and the building be of top quality.

Explaining the Text	*Examining the Text*
1. In this section Paul continued to build on one of the previous metaphors. He described the body of Christ as if it were a temple that was being built. And this temple (Christ's body) will be one that brings glory to Him.	1. Read 1 Corinthians 3:10-23. In what way did Paul lay the foundation for the church at Corinth? (v. 10)
	What particular care did he take? (v. 10)
	What care did he expect others to take? (vv. 10-11)
2. It is obvious that some building materials will survive testing by fire, whereas others will not. If the "materials" refer to spiritual works or labor contrasted with worldly works, then only the spiritu-	2. What kinds of material could be used to build on that foundation that had been laid? (v. 12)
	Describe some of the differences between the two categories of potential building materials.

Examining the Text	Explaining the Text
3. What will be the consequence of the testing that will be applied to the materials used in building Christ's body? (vv. 13-15)	al works will survive. If "materials" represent people, then the surviving materials represent Christians and the consumed represent non-Christians.
4. According to verse 16, how is a group of Christians (a church) different from any other miscellaneous gathering of people? How should we act toward a local group of believers? (v. 17)	4. The "you" in verse 16 is plural and probably refers to a local group of Christians (i.e., "a church") and should be received as a dire warning about doing anything that would contribute to the weakening or demise of a local church.
5. How do verses 18-23 summarize Paul's instructions about the church and how we should view it? What main ideas did Paul reiterate?	

C. VALID MINISTRY IN THE CHURCH *(1 Cor. 4:1-5).* If we were to ask various individuals what God expected of us as believers, we would receive many different answers. But here Paul gave a very simple answer. He clearly stated that God expects faithfulness.

Examining the Text	Explaining the Text
1. Read 1 Corinthians 4:1-5. How did Paul describe those who have been given the responsibility of leading? (v. 1)	1. The "us" in verse 1 probably refers back to those persons described in 3:22-23. Beyond the first-century ministers, this principle also could be extended to all of those

How Christians Ought to Act 25

Explaining the Text	*Examining the Text*
whom God has entrusted with positions of leadership.	What has been entrusted to them?
2. "Secret things of God" probably refers to those truths that God has revealed to us—the truths that we have received in the Bible. These are things that we could know in no other way, and thus they are secret things.	2. What does God expect of those leaders to whom He has entrusted His truth? (v. 2) How does this principle carry over into other areas of life?
3. Paul did not intend to communicate that what others think about us should be of no consequence. He did emphasize that in the final analysis, no human evaluation or judgment really matters.	3. Who were the three categories of persons that potentially could have passed judgment on Paul's ministry? (v. 3) How did Paul feel about being judged by those groups?
	4. In addition to the judgment of others, what else does not necessarily vindicate a leader before God? (v. 4) What does really matter?
5. The appointed time refers to the time that God judges (actually evaluates) all that we have done as believers. The purpose	5. When will God finally pass judgment on all that we have done? (v. 5)

Examining the Text	Explaining the Text
And what will be the result of that evaluation?	of this judgment is not to determine who is condemned and who has been justified, but it is an evaluation of our works as God's children—when God determines our rewards.

D. HUMILITY IN THE CHURCH *(1 Cor. 4:6-21).* Sometimes when others are trying to make themselves out to be much more than they really are, we respond with an ironic comment: "I wish that you really were all that you claim to be." In this section Paul responds to the Corinthians' presumption with just such irony.

Examining the Text	Explaining the Text
1. Read 1 Corinthians 4:6-21. What was the purpose in Paul's extensive teaching about himself and about the other ministers? (v. 6) What was the reason for not elevating one minister above another? (v. 7)	1. Even as Paul taught that human judgment (including his own self-evaluation) really doesn't matter, he also emphasized that the minor differences, to which we give great attention, also count for very little.
2. How did Paul sarcastically describe the Corinthian believers? (v. 8)	2. In their puffed-up and self-exalted state, the Corinthians had boasted great things and flaunted themselves. This generally was undeserved and was entirely inappropriate.
3. This entire section was written with a piercing, ironic tone. List the contrasts between how the Corinthians viewed themselves and the way in which the apostles served (vv. 9-13). *Corinthians* *Apostles*	3. Paul contrasted the way the Corinthian believers viewed themselves and wanted to be honored by others, with the self-deprecating manner in which the apostles served. The contrast is glaring and obvious.

How Christians Ought to Act

Explaining the Text	*Examining the Text*
	4. Why did Paul write to the Corinthians as he did? (vv. 14-15)
5. While Paul knew that he needed to present specific, blunt instructions to the Corinthians, he also knew that they needed a visual model whom they could observe and who could guide them.	5. What should the Corinthians have done rather than exalt themselves? (v. 16) How was Paul intending to help them? (v. 17)
6. Although Paul did not want to be harsh or judgmental, he knew that he had to address the selfish, carnal attitudes. And he was willing to do this even though it was an unpleasant task.	6. According to verse 18, what did some think about Paul's ministry? What did Paul actually intend to do? (v. 19) And how could he have come to them? (vv. 20-21)

Experiencing the Text

1. What metaphor (word picture) can you suggest that accurately pictures your church?

What could you do to promote a spirit of cooperation and encourage proper attitudes among your fellow Christians in your church?

2. In light of 1 Corinthians 3:1-23, write a summary sentence describing what a local church is, and how a believer should act as a member of that church.

3. Since all of us have been given responsibility by God, we must recognize Him as Judge. Ask Him to help you see yourself as He sees you, and write down any insights you receive concerning your own personal motivation.

4. What attitudes toward fellow Christians or the church could stand to be changed or corrected in your own life?

Write a brief prayer asking God to help you make those changes in your attitudes and subsequent actions.

STUDY THREE
1 Corinthians 5:1–6:20

Confronting Sin among Believers

Most of us find it very difficult to confront others. If a person has done something that we find unpleasant, we may complain to others about what that person has done. And we may even look for subtle ways to undermine that person's position or credibility. But when it comes to confronting that person directly, it's quite another matter.

Tom Peters, a well-known business consultant, recently has spoken and written about our failure to confront. Peters maintains that rather than confront others, we tolerate and even expect incompetence. Because of this we put up with badly designed and worse-serviced cars, appliances, and houses.

Recently my wife and I were dining with several other families at a very nice restaurant. We had made our reservations ahead of time and anticipated a lovely evening. But when we arrived, we discovered that nine places had been set at a six-person-sized table. The chairs touched each other even when they were pulled out.

When our waiter arrived, he communicated with us in monosyllabic grunts. Each request was received with thinly veiled intolerance. And to say that he was slow would be a dreadful understatement. He began his duties by serving the nine of us a basket containing only six slices of bread, and concluded the evening by grudgingly serving cold coffee with no offer of refills. What may be the worst part of all is that we not only failed to complain to the manager, but we permitted the restaurant to add the waiter's full tip to the bill.

In the church today, even as in first-century Corinth, we are prone to tolerate inappropriate behavior. What the Corinthians should have confronted and challenged, they accepted and even condoned. The church should confront unchristian behavior and deal with it appropriately. The guidelines in this passage help us understand appropriate behavior in confronting sin.

A. ATTITUDES TOWARD IMMORAL BROTHERS *(1 Cor. 5:1-13)*. All of us believers would like to know the right thing to do in every situation. Unfortunately, sometimes it is difficult to discern the proper choice. In this section Paul corrected the Corinthians for not rectifying a problem in the church that should have been an obvious decision.

Examining the Text

1. Read 1 Corinthians 5:1-13. What does Paul's expression "his father's wife" imply? (v. 1)

What do you think might have been Paul's tone of voice if he had expressed this statement out loud?

2. What was the Corinthian response to the situation? (v. 2)

What should it have been?

How did Paul respond to the flagrant sin? (v. 3)

3. How should the Corinthians have responded to the shameful way in which this believer was behaving? (vv. 2, 5)

4. What was the purpose of the radical course of action that Paul prescribed for the church to follow? (v. 5)

Explaining the Text

1. Apparently one of the Corinthian believers was living incestuously with his stepmother. This was forbidden in the Old Testament (Lev. 18:8). The Talmud prescribed stoning for the sin, and even Roman law (Cicero, Gaius) forbade it.

3. Fellowship among believers ought to have been significant and meaningful enough that to be deprived of it would have been a great personal loss for the believer.

4. "Handing over to Satan" apparently implied denying Christian fellowship and allowing the man to see his sin for what it really was (with the ultimate goal of restoration).

Confronting Sin among Believers

Explaining the Text	*Examining the Text*
5. Yeast often pictured sin. Part of the annual Passover ritual was getting rid of all yeast in the house, representing cleansing and purifying the home.	5. How does the influence of yeast in dough picture the influence that boasting has among believers? (vv. 6-7)
6. "Brother" was a common phrase used to identify a fellow believer, and did not necessarily refer to a blood relative. Among some believers today this expression commonly is employed.	6. What distinction did Paul make in warning the Christians not to have anything to do with sinners? (vv. 9-11) What standards of purity ought to apply within the church? (v. 11) 7. What is the obligation of local church leaders toward those who are in their church? (vv. 12-13)

B. LAWSUITS AMONG CHRISTIANS *(1 Cor. 6:1-8)*. How do you respond when someone hurts or offends you? Often the answer is "Sue them!" And it was in Corinth too. But Paul suggested a better way for believers to respond.

Explaining the Text	*Examining the Text*
1. Some people feel that the "disputes with one another" referred to conflicts over church matters alone, while others interpret this as being any conflict or argument among fellow Christians.	1. Read 1 Corinthians 6:1-8. What two ways did Paul suggest that lawsuits among believers could be settled? (vv. 1, 5-6) Which of these was more desirable? (v. 4)

Examining the Text	*Explaining the Text*
2. What rationale did Paul give to explain why Christians should appoint judges from among themselves? (vv. 2-3)	2. "Do you not know?" appears six times in this chapter (vv. 2, 3, 9, 15, 16, 19) and refers to obvious things that apparently the Corinthians had overlooked.
3. How would Paul have answered the objection that there were no wise or important men in the church who could have been appointed as judges? (v. 4)	
4. What is an alternative way (rather than appointing believers to judge specific disputes) to resolve conflict among believers? (vv. 7-8) Why do you think the Corinthians had not chosen this option?	4. In the U.S. today, one of the objectives of the Christian Legal Society (a fellowship of Christian attorneys) is to promote Christian conciliation, a means of resolving disputes among believers without resorting to the court system.

C. THE IMPORTANCE OF LEADING PURE LIVES *(1 Cor. 6:9-20)*. After addressing the problems of incest and of conflicts among believers, Paul turned to his other concerns about the lifestyle and general morality of the Corinthian believers.

Examining the Text	*Explaining the Text*
1. Read 1 Corinthians 6:9-20. Which sins on the list of those prevalent in Corinth are common in society today? (vv. 9-10) Can you identify any common thread that seems to run through this list?	1. Verse 9 could relate back to verse 1. "Wicked" (v. 9) is the same word as "ungodly" (v. 1). These words very aptly described those living in Corinth, a city notorious for its debauchery and immorality. Unfortunately this had infected the church too.

Confronting Sin among Believers

Explaining the Text

2. Apparently some of the Corinthians had been dominated by sins on this list prior to salvation ("And that is what some of you were," v. 11).

3. Some have suggested that the phrases in verses 12, 13, and 18 ("Everything is permissible," "Food for the stomach and the stomach for food," and "All . . . sins a man commits are outside his body" may have been sayings the Corinthians used to rationalize sin.

5. Paul's contention is that sexual immorality is a clear and obvious violation of our relationship with Christ. Since we have been purchased by Christ's death, even our bodies belong to God. Therefore, our physical behavior also should reflect spiritual truth.

Examining the Text

2. How had God dealt with these problems of the Corinthian believers? (v. 11)

3. What should be the limiting factor (for a believer) to keep liberty in perspective? (v. 12)

What keeps physical drives (desires for food and sex) in balance? (v. 13)

4. How are relationships in the physical realm a picture of our relationship with Christ? (vv. 14-17)

5. What is the reason that Paul gave to flee sexual impurity and immorality in verse 18?

What is the reason in verse 19?

What is the reason in verse 20?

Experiencing the Text

1. What general guidelines should we follow to insure purity and righteous living among believers in the church?

How can we avoid going to extremes that would result in a bitter, fault-finding attitude that hurts and condemns fellow believers?

2. Are there areas in your life where you feel that others have hurt or offended you? What are they?

How can you deal with them appropriately?

What do you need to do to correct things you have done that may have offended others?

3. Since your body as well as your spirit belongs to God, how does the way that you use your body (your physical behavior) reflect your spiritual commitment?

What might be areas where you need to modify your behavior?

Why not write out a brief prayer to God asking Him to help you behave in such a way that your physical behavior reflects your spiritual commitment?

STUDY FOUR
1 Corinthians 7:1-40

Christian Marriage Guidelines

Some years ago I was conducting a workshop at a local Sunday School convention. The planners of the convention wanted to have a series of workshops that presented the biblical guidelines for marriage. In one of these workshops, we had considered Genesis 2, a key passage describing the circumstances when God instituted marriage.

We had enjoyed a good time of examining several biblical passages and considering some appropriate applications for married people. As we neared the end of the hour, a young lady in the back of the room asked, "What about those of us who are not married? What does this passage have to say to us?"

Since the question really was beyond the scope of the workshop, I was tempted to suggest that we talk after dismissal, and, in the meantime, to answer someone else's question. But others seemed interested in the answer, and so I suggested that we look at 1 Corinthians 7. I pointed out several of the key principles in this passage. Particularly, I suggested that, while there are distinct advantages to being married, there also are some disadvantages.

I explained that most find fulfillment through a marriage partner. But then I explained that in some cases, God equips people for unique service that requires them to be single. I concluded by explaining that Paul indicated that God had given some people the gift of celibacy. With a snort that could be heard throughout the room, the young lady spat out, "Celibacy is not a gift; it's a curse."

After the laughter died down, I observed that if she felt that way, then God probably had not given her the gift of celibacy. I certainly hope that understanding the biblical guidelines enabled her to seek the quality of relationships that God had for her in life. And so we all need to know how God has called us. For this is the position in which we find true satisfaction and purpose.

A. GENERAL MARRIAGE GUIDELINES *(1 Cor. 7:1-9).* Often we hear children say things like "It's my toy; I'll do what I want with it." When they grow older it may take the form, "It's my body; I'll do what I want with it." But Paul clearly contradicted this immature assertion. A married person's body also belongs to that person's spouse, which should influence both attitudes and behavior.

Examining the Text	*Explaining the Text*
1. Read 1 Corinthians 7:1-9. In light of the questions the Corinthians had asked, what was Paul's statement concerning celibacy (remaining unmarried and not sexually active)? (v. 1)	1. The first phrase of 7:1 indicates that Paul's statements were responses to specific questions from Corinth. While we don't have the exact questions, they probably related to the moral/religious climate there.
2. What seems to be a problem that complicated living a celibate life in Corinth? (v. 2) According to verse 2, what should be the only alternative to celibacy?	
3. How should a man view his own body in relation to his wife? (vv. 3-4) And how should a woman view hers? (vv. 3-4)	3. Regular sexual relationships are a normal part of marriage, indeed a necessary part. Apparently some Corinthians were trying to practice sexual abstinence within marriage, acting as if they were celibate.
4. What four guidelines did Paul give to guide husbands and wives in abstinence from regular sexual intercourse? (v. 5)	4. Clearly, sexual intercourse practiced on a regular basis (the actual frequency is not mentioned, but apparently it should be acceptable to both

Christian Marriage Guidelines

Explaining the Text	*Examining the Text*
spouses) is a normal and necessary part of the marriage relationship as God designed it.	Would you say that abstinence is necessary or optional? (v. 6)
5. Some feel that Paul had been married and was a widower, or that perhaps his wife left him when he became a Christian.	5. Why do you think it was good that Paul remained unmarried? What was one major problem in remaining unmarried? (vv. 8-9)
6. Paul probably was addressing these comments to those who had been married and, therefore, were sexually experienced (i.e., widows, widowers, divorced people). These would have faced intense pressure in Corinth due to sexual looseness there.	6. Which of the two options that Paul presented is appropriate for the average person? (vv. 8-9) What does it take to "override" the drives that God has built into people? (v. 7)

B. MARRIAGE AND DIVORCE *(1 Cor. 7:10-24).* There are few topics that are any more relevant to people living today than the biblical guidelines for marriage and divorce. Divorce has reached epidemic proportions, and in the midst of all the confusion we need to consider God's expectations.

Explaining the Text	*Examining the Text*
1. Throughout this passage, Paul periodically distinguished between what he was saying and what the Lord said. This doesn't imply any less authority, or suggest that it is merely Paul's opinion. Paul clarified which parts of the message (revealed to him by the Holy Spirit) were given	1. Read 1 Corinthians 7:10-24. What basic principles summarized Paul's teaching about divorce and remarriage? (vv. 10-11)

Examining the Text	Explaining the Text
	to supplement the teaching that Jesus gave while He was living on the earth. Both Paul's and Jesus' teaching were authoritative.
2. What if a believer is married to an unbeliever who is willing to remain married? (vv. 12-13)	
What if the unbeliever insists on a divorce? (v. 15)	
3. What is the positive element in a marriage where one spouse has turned to Christ, but the other one has not? (vv. 14, 16)	3. "Has been sanctified" (literally, "has been set apart") does not mean the person is a believer, but that a special measure of grace will flow from God through the believing spouse.
4. What is the obligation of the believing partner if the unbelieving spouse insists on a divorce? (v. 15)	4. "Is not bound" may indicate that the believer is free to remarry. However, some feel that it means the believer is free of obligation to try to maintain the marriage—not necessarily to remarry.
What is one of God's ultimate goals for each and every marriage relationship? (v. 15)	
5. What is the most important factor in determining what we do and how we live? (v. 17)	5. Apparently, some of the Corinthians were teaching that a person who accepted Christ had to leave a partner, or get married, or make some other radical change.
What basic guideline does this have to agree with? (v. 19)	

Christian Marriage Guidelines

Explaining the Text	*Examining the Text*
	6. In addition to married/unmarried, what are some other circumstances in which people have found themselves when they accepted Christ?
	How could this influence the way in which they might be able to minister?

C. MARRIAGE AND MINISTRY *(1 Cor. 7:25-35)*. There is no question that God has created us with a need for companionship. And He has given us physical drives to reinforce our desires. But for certain ministries, God may call individuals to celibacy for His purposes.

Explaining the Text	*Examining the Text*
1. "Virgins" probably refers to anyone who is sexually inexperienced (i.e., unmarried, celibate). Paul indicated that, in light of impending persecution, there were advantages to remaining single.	1. Read 1 Corinthians 7:25-35. What is the first reason that Paul gave to explain the benefits of celibacy (remaining single)? (vv. 26, 28b) Which of the two options (marriage or celibacy) is acceptable? (vv. 27-28)
2. These explanations of how people view life seem to focus on the fact that it is temporary, short-lived, and we are looking for eternity.	2. What is the second reason that would commend celibacy to a believer? (vv. 29-31)
3. Paul did not condemn spouses for considering each other. He stated it as a fact of how God has created us and expects us to live.	3. What is the third reason that would commend celibacy? (vv. 32, 35)

Examining the Text	Explaining the Text
4. What obligations do married people have toward each other? (vv. 32-34)	
5. What freedoms do unmarried people have? (v. 35)	5. Apparently, some had distorted Paul's teaching and had been advocating divorce so they could minister. Paul dispelled this error in verses 17-24.

D. ATTITUDE TOWARD MARRIAGE *(1 Cor. 7:36-40).* It's all too easy to take a portion of what someone has said and consider it out of context. Perhaps that is why Paul concluded this section with a reiteration of basic principles that we should observe in marriage.

Examining the Text	Explaining the Text
1. Read 1 Corinthians 7:36-40. What two possibilities exist for a man (either an engaged man to his fiancée or a father toward his daughter) in his attitude toward the unmarried woman? (v. 37)	1. "He is engaged to" is an interpretation added by the NIV translators. The meaning also could be "his virgin daughter" (see *Bible Knowledge Commentary, New Testament,* p. 520).
2. Which option did Paul indicate was right? (v. 38)	2. In trying to interpret verses 38 and 40 it is helpful to recall 1 Corinthians 7:1, 26, and 29. There were immediate circumstances that influenced what was best for the Corinthians to do.
Which did he recommend? (v. 38)	
Why do you think he recommended it? (v. 39)	
3. How long does the marriage bond exist? (v. 39)	

Christian Marriage Guidelines

Explaining the Text	*Examining the Text*
	What happens if a spouse dies? (v. 39)
	4. What limitation did Paul place on the believer who chooses to remarry? (v. 39)
	What was Paul's personal preference? (v. 40)

Experiencing the Text

1. What obligations do we who are married have in the way that we use our time and our bodies?

What are some of the benefits and ministry advantages for those who are unmarried?

2. In what ways would it be appropriate to modify your behavior based on Paul's teachings in chapter 7?

3. What distinct advantages do you have in your personal or vocational life that equip you uniquely to serve God?

Take time right now and thank God for the position that He has called you to in life. Ask Him for wisdom to know how to use it for His glory.

STUDY FIVE
1 Corinthians 8:1–9:27

Christian Rights and Obligations

In recent months, good friends of ours have been going through the "empty nest syndrome." This is the time when children leave home in order to establish their own families. Elaine and I have observed attentively, anticipating similar experiences in the next few years.

There are at least two significant aspects to the experience. Obviously, husband and wife need to establish new routines and expectations. As the children were growing up, much of the daily routine and many choices were determined by what was best for the children. But finally, they no longer are a key factor.

Another issue that a couple has to face is the whole matter of "letting go." We parents have to realize that we have done our jobs, now granting our children the freedom to establish new families. And we also grant them full responsibility for their decisions, hoping that they will have learned to become responsible through our guidance.

One key time when we can observe how well we are teaching personal accountability comes when our children become old enough to drive the car. This is when we can see if our teens recognize that when they earn a driver's license, it involves far more than just new privileges. Along with the obvious privileges, there is responsibility—responsibility to operate the automobile in a safe, legal manner. And the obligation to monitor critical supplies of gasoline and oil. But most important, when they slip behind the steering wheel, they also assume critical responsibility for the welfare of anyone else in the car.

In many areas of life, responsibility is linked with privilege. If we have the privilege of living in a community, we also have obligations to that community. As Christians, we have many rights and privileges. But we also have obligations. And we cannot truly enjoy the rights that come with believing in Christ unless we also are willing to consider the obligations that accompany those rights.

Christian Rights and Obligations

A. CHRISTIAN LIBERTY AND LIMITATION *(1 Cor. 8:1-13)*.

When we were children, most of us had no idea that our parents sacrificed for us. Even though our parents had rights and privileges, frequently they relinquished them for us. As believers we ought to be equally willing to do what is best for younger Christians.

Explaining the Text	*Examining the Text*
1. "Now about food offered to idols" parallels "Now for the matters" (7:1) and indicates this was one of their questions. Since the best meat often was offered to idols before selling, some wondered whether Christians should eat it or not.	1. Read 1 Corinthians 8:1-13. What two personal qualities did Paul contrast? (v. 1) What result does each of these two qualities produce in our lives? (v. 1)
2. Apparently thinking one knows something (v. 2) refers to an elementary level of knowledge that does not entail true understanding.	2. What is more important than merely knowing something that is true? (vv. 2-3)
3. The teaching about idols has been included here as important background to the Christian living principles that the Corinthians needed to know. Since the nature of idols was the key to understanding eating meat, Paul first provided theological instruction.	3. What are contrasting descriptions that Paul made between the one true God and all of the idols (false gods)? (vv. 4-6) *True God* *Idols (False Gods)*
	4. How did those with incomplete understanding feel about eating meat that first had been offered to idols? (v. 7)

Examining the Text

What would have happened to their consciences if they had gone ahead and eaten that food?

5. What is a mature believer's proper understanding of the food that first had been offered to false gods? (v. 8)

6. What would a person who understands that idols are nothing think about eating meat that had been offered as a sacrifice? (vv. 8-9)

How could this affect a less mature Christian with a weak conscience? (vv. 10-11)

7. What did Paul suggest the more mature believer should do if there were the possibility of offending a less mature believer? (v. 13)

8. Why did Paul consider the welfare of the weaker brother to be so important? (v. 12)

In the situations that Paul described in this chapter, which of the personal qualities (v. 1) would take precedence?

Explaining the Text

6. The danger that Paul was concerned about was the very real possibility of a less mature believer modeling behavior after a more mature one. The less mature might copy the behavior but still feel guilty, thus violating the dictates of his own conscience.

7. "Fall into sin" means causing a weaker brother to revert to a previous life of sinful behavior. It involves more than someone simply disagreeing with another on an issue.

Christian Rights and Obligations

B. THE RIGHTS OF AN APOSTLE *(1 Cor. 9:1-18).* After hearing chapter 8 read, it is very logical that a Corinthian believer might have reacted indignantly. "Why should I give up my rights for another, especially a weaker person?" Paul countered with chapter 9. "Consider what I have given up as an apostle."

Explaining the Text	*Examining the Text*
1. This entire chapter could be read in a very defensive tone of voice. However, it also could be read with a tone of grieving. Paul was not defending himself. Rather, he was using himself as an example to help believers understand proper attitudes.	1. Read 1 Corinthians 9:1-18. What four questions did Paul ask (rhetorically, we assume) in verse 1? What is the answer to all of these questions? In what way would Paul have been special to the Corinthians? (v. 2, cp. 1:6; 2:1; 3:10)
	2. What rights could Paul (and Barnabas) have exercised? (vv. 3-6) How might they have felt about the limitations imposed by not exercising those rights?
3. Paul's line of argument was that in many other areas of life it is normal for the worker to receive support based on the labor that he provides. Even the Mosaic Law commanded that the oxen should be allowed to benefit from the work that they do (Deut. 25:4).	3. In verses 7-10, what six analogies (comparisons) did Paul use to explain how he and Barnabas could have expected to be supported by those to whom they ministered?

Examining the Text	*Explaining the Text*
4. How did the principle of support apply directly to Paul and Barnabas? (vv. 11-12)	4. It is important to recognize that Paul was not complaining, rather illustrating how Christians can relinquish their rights for others.
5. What material support for those ministering was provided under the Mosaic system? (v. 13) According to verse 14, what principle related to preaching the Gospel?	5. Although we know of no such explicit command, there may be teachings of Christ that have not been preserved for us, or Paul may have been referring to the principle from a passage such as Luke 10:5-7.
6. What motivation could some have attributed to Paul for writing this passage? (v. 15) In verses 16-18, what was Paul's motivation for preaching? How can his motivation be an example to us today?	6. Rather than be accused of improper motivation, Paul wanted to clarify that his driving force in life, that which motivated him, was preaching the Gospel. All other desires seem to have been controlled by this overwhelming goal.

C. FOCUSING ON WHAT IS REALLY IMPORTANT *(1 Cor. 9:19-27)*. It is easy for us to start a task only to realize sometime later that we have gotten sidetracked. The original task has been laid aside because some other project has captured our attention. Paul was determined not to let this happen in his ministry.

Christian Rights and Obligations

Explaining the Text	*Examining the Text*
	1. Read 1 Corinthians 9:19-27. What driving principle had captivated Paul? (v. 19)
2. It is important to realize that Paul was not compromising his spiritual principles. Rather, he allowed his personal preferences to be determined by what was important to those receiving his ministry. He met people where they were.	2. In what ways did Paul vary his approach so that he could relate more effectively to certain groups? (vv. 20-22)
	3. What sports analogies did Paul cite to explain how he disciplined himself in order to minister as effectively as possible? (vv. 24-26)
4. Paul's emphasis on his body (physical needs and drives) probably relates back to, and extends his earlier explanation about, attitudes toward receiving material support as a minister to the Corinthians.	4. How could Paul's physical, bodily needs (v. 27) get in the way of his spiritual ministry? How has the desire for physical benefits proved to be an obstruction to the Gospel ministry in our time?

Experiencing the Text

1. What principles growing out of Paul's teaching in chapter 8 should guide our behavior in relationships today?

What are some potential areas where we could offend (cause to revert to a previous life of sin) a brother or sister in Christ?

What should we, who might be free, do about our behavior in such areas?

2. How do you feel about giving up your rights for a fellow Christian, especially one who is weaker (less mature)?

For whom are you really giving them up if you choose to limit your freedom?

3. Are there persons ministering to you who ought to be receiving more generous material support, based on the principle of providing for those who minister?

4. What personal preferences in neutral areas (those that are neither commanded nor forbidden) have you relinquished in order to minister to others?

What things might you need to give up in the future?

5. Evaluate which are the areas in which your physical desires might hinder growth. Take time to pray and ask God to help you control those drives and desires.

STUDY SIX

1 Corinthians 10:1–11:1

When Christians Disagree

Quite a few years ago I was working with a group of high school young people. This was about the time when long hair was becoming increasingly popular—with the young people. Unfortunately, many of the adults did not fully appreciate a very full head of hair.

One of the fellows in the group had begun wearing his hair somewhat longer than in the past. But one of the deacons in the church could not stand the sight of this teenager's hair. And so he began teasing the young man. He called the teenager "dear" and "sweetie." It came to the place where the young man actually dreaded coming to church because of what he (and I) considered harassment.

In one of our youth Bible studies, we were examining 1 Corinthians 10. We discussed the principle of the stronger Christian adapting his behavior to the understanding of the weaker Christian. We discussed that while some things might be perfectly acceptable, if they offended a weak Christian, a truly mature believer could choose not to do them.

I tried to present several illustrations to show how the principle applies to us today. One of the illustrations that I chose was hairstyle. Even though a person might be able to wear his hair longer, if it offended another Christian, that person also might choose *not* to wear it long.

The teenager explained that whether his hair was long or short didn't matter all that much. However, he felt that if the deacon really was offended, he could just as easily have it cut shorter. But as he said that, the teenager's eyes lit up. "That means," he said, "if I cut my hair so as not to offend him, I'm the stronger Christian and he's the weaker one. That's really cool." The young man had grasped a concept that many older Christians still struggle with. Even though certain things might be no problem to us, we still have an obligation to think about how we will influence others. And if our behavior would offend another, we have the privilege of giving up our rights for the welfare of that person.

A. OBEDIENCE TO CHRIST *(1 Cor. 10:1-13)*. Most of us have heard that experience is the best teacher. Someone observed that the main problem with experience is that she gives the exam before teaching the lesson. But we can learn from the experience of others. In fact, God intends for us to learn from Israel's experience.

Examining the Text	*Explaining the Text*
1. Read 1 Corinthians 10:1-13. What is the purpose of giving us the record of what Israel did? (vv. 6, 11)	
2. What special benefits did the Israelites receive from God? (vv. 1-4)	2. "The spiritual rock" is a reference to the source where God told Moses to get water in the wilderness. It is a picture (type) of Christ.
3. In spite of all of the benefits that God provided for Israel, what was the experience of almost all of the Israelites who left Egypt? (v. 5) Which ones did not die in the wilderness? (Num. 14:29-31)	3. The reason why most of the Israelites died is found in Numbers 13:21–14:24.
4. Even as the Israelites missed out on the blessing of God, we could have a similar experience today. In what ways could we miss the blessing of God?	
5. What four things did the Israelites do that were in direct disobedience to God's command? (vv. 7-10)	5. Even though the Israelites were God's chosen people, when they disobeyed they suffered the

Explaining the Text	*Examining the Text*
consequences of disobedience. For further explanation, see the *Bible Knowledge Commentary, New Testament*, pp. 526–527.	
	6. What warning did Paul give the believers, based on what happened to Israel? (v. 10)
	How could we become complacent and presumptuous? (v. 12)
7. All of us human beings are susceptible to similar temptation. We should recognize that we have the same tendencies that Israel had and should seek to avoid repeating their sin.	7. What has God promised us about the temptations that we face? (v. 13)

B. COMMITMENT TO CHRIST *(1 Cor. 10:14-22).* It is very important for us to realize that when we accepted Christ as Saviour, we also accepted obligations. Just as God is faithful to us, He expects us to be faithful in our commitment to Him. One of the symbols of this relationship is the observance of the Lord's Supper.

Explaining the Text	*Examining the Text*
	1. Read 1 Corinthians 10:14-22. What does the "therefore" that begins verse 14 indicate about the relationship of the following verses to what went before?

Examining the Text	*Explaining the Text*
What did Paul expect those who read his letter to do about his teaching? (v. 15)	
2. What two specific symbols did Paul choose to explain the deep identification with Christ? (vv. 16-17) What further truth does the picture of the Lord's Supper illustrate? (v. 17)	2. Frequently throughout the Bible, God described idolatry (His children following after pagan gods) as spiritual adultery. In this passage, the Lord's Supper is symbolic of our identification with Christ, and any other worship would be considered spiritual adultery.
3. How were the sacrifices that the Israelites made different from pagan sacrifices? (v. 18)	3. In the Old Testament sacrificial system, there was strong identification between offering a sacrifice and the reality behind that sacrifice.
4. What is an idol? (v. 19) What is the reality behind idols? (v. 20)	
5. What two possible actions of the Corinthians were totally incompatible? (v. 21) Why were these incompatible?	5. "Table of demons" refers to the offering of sacrifices to demonic powers through the idols that represented those demons.
6. According to verse 22, why would idol worship arouse God's jealousy?	6. Although we view human jealousy as a negative trait, a holy God has every right to demand absolute loyalty and to punish spiritual adultery.

When Christians Disagree

C. SERVICE TO CHRIST *(1 Cor. 10:23–11:1)*.

Most of us who are parents or who have worked with young people have heard the question "It's my life; why can't I do with it as I please?" But we are responsible for more than just ourselves. We also must consider our impact on others.

Explaining the Text	*Examining the Text*
1. Freedom in Christ involves a recognition of the fact that there are many areas of life where God has not commanded that either we should or should not do something. These are areas where we must make decisions on the basis of biblical principles.	1. Read 1 Corinthians 10:23–11:1. What two significant restrictions should we place on our freedom? (v. 23) What guideline can we apply to help us decide what behavior is appropriate? (v. 24)
2. Even though much of the meat that was sold in the market had been offered to idols, this did not change the essential nature or quality of that meat.	2. According to verse 26, what is the reason that one could eat meat that has been sold in the market without fear of sinning? 3. What should a Christian do when confronted with the possibility of doing something when there is no known problem with that behavior? (v. 27) What implications might this have for those who are afraid of doing wrong unknowingly?
4. A "weaker brother" is one who is less mature than another and does not understand freedom in a given area. This person would be encouraged to violate conscience by doing something that seems to be wrong to that person.	4. In a questionable situation, two attitudes are possible. What would be appropriate if you were in the presence of a weaker Christian? (vv. 28-29) What might be one's behavior if no one else will be affected? (v. 30)

Examining the Text

5. What key factors in our relationship with God should control our behavior? (vv. 30-31)

6. What key factors in our relationship with others also influence what we do? (10:32–11:1)

Explaining the Text

5. Paul extended the principle beyond eating meat and applied it to all areas of life. What we do is important, but the attitude with which we do it is even more important.

Experiencing the Text

1. What personal warning do you receive from the negative example of Israel?

What could you do to encourage faithful obedience to what God expects of you?

2. Even though few of us ever would worship pagan idols, other things can draw us away from God. What things could become idols that replace God in your time and devotion?

How could you prevent that from happening?

3. What are some areas where you have observed Christians disagreeing on what is proper and improper behavior?

How do they resolve such conflict?

4. What are some activities that could be morally neutral and yet still offend another Christian who might be less mature?

How will you choose to behave in those areas?

STUDY SEVEN
1 Corinthians 11:2-34

Celebrating Jesus' Sacrifice

Several years ago I visited India to minister in a series of Christian Education conferences sponsored by the Evangelical Fellowship of India. I was there in late September and early October, during one of the many Indian religious festivals. This one happened to be a Hindu festival in honor of Ganesh, the elephant god, a god of prosperity.

The first thing I noticed about the celebration was the music being played. Even before I saw any of the festivities, from a great distance I could hear the amplified "noise." Throughout the city faithful Hindus had set up booths, each with an image of the elephant god. And they were playing music to honor this god.

Throughout the day and the night, the faithful came to make offerings to this god—a god of prosperity. And while many had little to give, they came in steady streams, hoping to receive their god's favor. Late into the night they came, celebrating and making supplication.

The days of celebrating ended with an all-night party of singing, dancing and drinking, culminating in a raucous march through the streets. The faithful, who had decorated their faces with fluorescent pink powder, threw handfuls of the powder on passersby in the street. In every city the parades ended at a lake or river where the worshipers "drowned" the image in a final frenzied climax—"the immersion of Ganesh."

The contrast between this celebration and Christianity was obvious to me and to the other Christians. Our celebration is not drunken revelry. Rather than giving us a thinly veiled reason for indulging in excess, Christ has transformed us internally so that our behavior is changed. This is not to say that we have no celebration. But when we celebrate the Lord's Supper, we focus on the completed work of Christ. Unfortunately, the Corinthians brought more than a little pagan celebration into the Lord's Supper. And as Paul tried to correct their misunderstanding, he also gave guidelines for proper observance.

A. APPROPRIATE WORSHIP *(1 Cor. 11:2-16)*. Many of the questions and issues that currently concern us in the local church also were of concern in first-century Corinth. What is proper behavior, and how do we show proper attitudes? These questions are just as important today as they were in the first century.

Examining the Text	*Explaining the Text*
1. Read 1 Corinthians 11:2-16. For what reason was Paul able to praise the believers in Corinth? (v. 2)	1. This whole chapter deals with guidelines for church worship. Verses 2-16 reflect the fact that Paul selected godly men to lead in the churches.
2. What is the order of authority within the local church? (v. 3)	2. It is important to recognize that in the church, submission is a principle that applies to everyone, not just a few. Christ, men, and women all are under authority.
3. What is the appropriate manner in which a Corinthian man was to pray or prophesy (teach)? (v. 4) What was the appropriate manner in which a Corinthian woman was to pray or prophesy (teach)? (v. 5)	3. In the first century, a head covering indicated that a person was subject to the leadership of another who was physically present. In the worship service, since men were physically present, women wore a covering; but, since Christ was not physically present, the men did not.
4. If a woman prayed or taught without a head covering, she was disgraced. What would have been a further symbol of disgrace? (v. 6)	

Celebrating Jesus' Sacrifice

Explaining the Text	*Examining the Text*
5. The theological reason is based on the order that was established at Creation. The source passages for the two-part reason are Genesis 2:18 and 23.	5. What is the two-part theological reason that men were assigned responsibility for giving direction within the church? (vv. 8-9)
6. Apparently, angels observe us; and even as some originally rebelled, those who observe improper church relationships still could be encouraged to rebel against God's authority.	6. What is another reason that believers should show proper attitudes toward leadership and that these believers need to respond properly toward authority? (v. 10)
	7. As a balancing principle, what generally is the male/female relationship? (vv. 11-12)
8. Some feel that "nature" relates to their assumption that a man's hair will not grow as long as a woman's. Others feel that "nature" is the natural order, i.e., society's accepted patterns with men wearing shorter hair.	8. Beyond the spiritual principle, what reinforces the idea that a woman could show submission to leadership by having her head covered? (vv. 13-15)
9. Perhaps the concluding statement is to emphasize that specific customs are not as significant as the fact that they show key attitudes toward spiritual leadership—a very important topic.	9. What seems to be the overall emphasis throughout these verses (vv. 2-16) in relation to order within the local church?

B. ERRORS IN OBSERVING THE LORD'S SUPPER *(1 Cor. 11:17-22)*. In some cases, the very programs and procedures that should draw people together actually separate and alienate them. In the Corinthian church it was the Lord's Supper observance that produced schism.

Examining the Text	*Explaining the Text*
1. Read 1 Corinthians 11:17-22. What seems to be the attitude with which Paul wrote this section?	1. The memorial that was intended to be a meaningful unifying experience had become negative, and even divisive, among the believers.
2. What had Paul heard about the Corinthian worship experiences? (v. 18) Do you think that Paul believed everything that he had heard? Why or why not?	2. Paul used the phrase "in the first place" to call attention to a key idea. It doesn't necessarily indicate the first in a list of things.
3. Why had the Lord's Supper become a meaningless observance for the Corinthians? (vv. 20-21)	3. Apparently, rather than sharing food at the Lord's Supper, each person ate whatever he had brought. Some had much while others had none and went hungry.
4. What should the Corinthians have done if they weren't going to share? (v. 22) What would have been even better?	
5. What was the net result of the Corinthians' behavior? (v. 22)	5. It is quite ironic that the very observance commemorating Christ's sacrifice was reflecting selfishness and lack of consideration for others.

Celebrating Jesus' Sacrifice

C. PROPER OBSERVANCE OF THE LORD'S SUPPER *(1 Cor. 11:23-34).* Although there are very few rituals in Christianity, compared to other religions, the Lord's Supper is an intensely moving memorial with deep symbolism. And it should be observed properly, particularly with the proper attitude on the part of each Christian.

Explaining the Text

1. The historical event that set the precedent for this observance was Jesus' final Passover supper with the apostles (Matt. 26:17-30; Mark 14:12-26; Luke 22:7-23). But since Paul was not an apostle at that time, apparently Jesus revealed this to Paul at a later time (cp. Gal. 1:11-12).

3. "In an unworthy manner" also could be translated "in a careless manner." This would be taking the Lord's Supper worship lightly or carelessly.

4. Many interpreters feel that the term "have fallen asleep" (v. 30) may refer to believers who actually have died due to the judgment of God on them for carelessness or irreverence in the Lord's Supper celebration.

Examining the Text

1. Read 1 Corinthians 11:23-34. What was the source of Paul's information? (v. 23)

What two key elements were to be used in celebrating the Lord's Supper and what did they represent? (vv. 23-25)

2. What is a key reason for celebrating the Lord's Supper? (v. 26)

3. But what solemn warning did Paul also give regarding this celebration? (v. 27)

4. According to verses 29, what is the danger of participating carelessly?

And what could be the consequences? (v. 30)

Examining the Text

5. What can believers do to avoid the potential judgment for careless participation? (vv. 28, 31)

According to verse 32, what will happen if we don't judge ourselves?

6. How could the Corinthians have avoided the problems that they had experienced with the Lord's Supper celebration? (vv. 33-34)

Explaining the Text

6. The principle is clear. Believers who treat each other with scorn or with lack of consideration actually are offending Christ.

Experiencing the Text

1. In what ways do we tend to show improper relationships or attitudes toward leaders in the church today?

What can we do to encourage Christians to model proper behavior?

2. What are some of the divisive elements that may exist in your church?

How could these be corrected to show Christian unity?

3. In what ways might we be guilty of sinning against Christ by our attitudes toward fellow Christians?

4. What does the death and the subsequent resurrection of Christ mean to you?

How do you show it?

STUDY EIGHT

1 Corinthians 12:1-31

Believers Equipped for Service

It is highly enlightening to examine popular advertising themes. Corporations pay advertising agencies large sums of money to design and implement effective advertising campaigns. These agencies must devise strategies that will persuade consumers to part with their hard-earned money to secure products or services.

Naturally a key element in all of this is determining what concepts will provide sufficient motivation for us to spend our money. Apparently, the concepts that are used to motivate us do work, since they are used repeatedly, for many different products.

One popular motivator is the common desire to be famous. Advertisers work to convince us that a celebrity uses a particular product. The implication is that by using that same product, we somehow can identify with the fame of that person who endorses the product.

Another theme is the appeal to status. Driving a particular car or wearing a particular cologne will set you apart from the common, ordinary people. This particular product will let everyone know that you are "somebody."

The "bandwagon" is another theme that is overworked. The idea is that everyone uses this particular product, and you certainly wouldn't want to be left out, would you? In actuality we should consider it a privilege not to be part of the "everybody" who is risking lung cancer, alcoholism, or bankruptcy.

While the phenomenon of consumer advertising may be fairly recent, the motivations certainly are not. The Corinthians struggled with many of the same desires. They wanted to identify with famous people. They also were concerned with status. And none of them wanted to be left out. Because of these desires, many viewed their place in the church from a totally wrong perspective. In this chapter, Paul wrote to correct many of these misimpressions.

The First Epistle to the Corinthians

A. BELIEVERS AND SPIRITUAL GIFTS *(1 Cor. 12:1-6).* Perhaps you have heard the expression, "I'm not all that I should be, but I thank the Lord that I'm not what I used to be." This was the condition of the Corinthians. They had progressed from idol worship, but still had a long way to go.

Examining the Text

1. Read 1 Corinthians 12:1-6. What did Paul state was the major theme of this section? (v. 1)

   What seemed to be his major concern? (v. 1)

2. Why do you think that Paul felt it was important to teach believers about spiritual gifts?

   What had been the Corinthians' condition before they responded to the Gospel? (v. 2)

3. What seems to be the basic "spiritual gift" that God's Spirit bestows on believers? (v. 3)

4. What are some of the things that contribute to individual differences in our ministries as believers? (vv. 4-6)

5. In contrast with the differences among believers, what things do we have in common? (vv. 4-6)

Explaining the Text

1. "Now about" indicates that Paul was moving to address another topic that he wanted to consider in this letter to the Corinthian church.

2. Apparently even though the Corinthians believed in Jesus Christ, they still were confused about many of the principles of growth and maturity, bringing some of their old views into Christianity.

3. Saying "Jesus is Lord" rather than "Jesus is cursed" is an affirmation reflecting the enlightening work of the Holy Spirit.

4. "Gifts" comes from the Greek word *charis* which means "grace." They are "gifts of grace" or "grace gifts."

5. While it is true that we have many things in common, those who follow Christ also play unique roles

Believers Equipped for Service

Explaining the Text	*Examining the Text*
in the body of Christ. And the body is only healthy when we use those gifts to serve.	Why do you think that Paul began this discussion of spiritual gifts by explaining what we have in common?

B. VARIATIONS IN GIFTS *(1 Cor. 12:7-11).* There are few messages that need to be heard more today than the truth that we all have individual roles in the church. As people struggle to establish their identities and to be individuals, we need to help them see that the Holy Spirit has equipped them for just that purpose.

Explaining the Text	*Examining the Text*
1. "Manifestation of the Spirit" refers to visible expressions of the Holy Spirit's power at work in believers' lives.	1. Read 1 Corinthians 12:7-11. What is the reason for which the Holy Spirit distributes spiritual gifts? (v. 7)
2. This is not an exhaustive list of spiritual gifts, but these were some of the more dramatic gifts. Many Bible scholars feel that some of the gifts were given for the establishment of the early church but did not continue (see 1 Cor. 13:8-10; cp. Eph. 2:20).	2. What are the nine gifts listed in this section, and what could have been their contribution to the early church? (vv. 8-10) *Gift* *Contribution*

Examining the Text	*Explaining the Text*
3. According to verse 11, what is the common source of all of these gifts?	
4. On what basis were the gifts distributed? (v. 11)	4. The word "man" was supplied by the translators. The Greek text reads "to each" and we could supply "one" (NASB) or "person."

C. UNITY IN SPIRITUAL GIFTS *(1 Cor. 12:12-26).* How many times have we looked at another person and wished that we had the skills or abilities of that individual? It is likely that same person was looking at us and feeling similar longings about different features. Unfortunately, that's how the Corinthians felt about spiritual gifts. And Paul clarified the importance of diversity in the body.

Examining the Text	*Explaining the Text*
1. Read 1 Corinthians 12:12-26. What analogy (comparison) did Paul make to explain the nature of the church (those who believe in Christ)? (v. 12)	
2. What common experience do all believers share? (v. 13) How is this fact a great "equalizer" among believers? (v. 13)	2. Spirit baptism occurs when one becomes a member of the body of Christ, receiving the Holy Spirit at the moment of salvation. The Greek grammar shows that it took place at that time. In contrast, "filling" occurs subsequent to salvation (Eph. 5:18).

Believers Equipped for Service

Explaining the Text	*Examining the Text*
3. Paul painted a dramatic picture to illustrate this teaching. Imagine an entire person who was nothing but a giant ear. Equally absurd is that each believer would try to play exactly the same role within the church.	3. In one or two sentences summarize the basic teaching about each believer's position and role within the body of Christ (vv. 14-20).
	4. What keeps all believers from becoming isolated, individual entities? (v. 20)
	On what basis has the assignment of roles been made? (vv. 18-19)
5. One of the Corinthian problems was self-centeredness (even as in the church today). Paul wanted to help the Corinthians (and us) to become more concerned for others.	5. According to verse 21, what warning should we heed as Christians?
6. The parts of our body that are most critical to health and life are not seen but are covered. They are covered with the exterior parts of the body that are seen, which serve to protect those fragile parts that are so important.	6. What extremely important parts are critical to the effective functioning of our physical bodies, even though those parts are not visible in their working?
	How does this help us to understand the healthy functioning of the spiritual body of Christ? (vv. 22-23)
7. The idea that one member would seek to receive special honor or glory for contributing ministry to the body is totally foreign to the purpose of these grace gifts.	7. What truths should keep believers with less visible gifts from feeling unimportant? (vv. 24-25)
	How does each believer share in the life of the body of Christ? (v. 26)

D. SIGNIFICANCE OF GIFTS *(1 Cor. 12:27-31)*.

Many people are "hung up" on status. They think it comes from material possessions or playing significant roles. But for the Christian, true status comes from serving. And the goal of serving in this position is to give, not to receive.

Examining the Text

1. Read 1 Corinthians 12:27-31. Why do you think the first three gifts mentioned here played such an important role in the early church? (v. 28)

2. What gift did Paul place at the bottom of the list? (v. 28)

3. How do verses 29-30 build on and explain the previous section?

4. On what basis would any desired gift be a "greater" gift if the goal of spiritual gifts is to build a strong, unified body? (v. 31)

Explaining the Text

1. In this list "first, second, third" probably refers to the rank of importance in ministry to the entire church. The Corinthians had elevated the last one to first place.

3. Each of the questions in verses 29-30 is phrased in Greek so as to expect a "no" answer. (E.g., "They aren't all apostles, are they?")

Experiencing the Text

1. Why is it important for you as a believer to recognize what you have in common with other Christians?

And why is it equally important to recognize diversity or variation?

2. In what ways has God's Holy Spirit prepared you for service so that you are uniquely equipped to minister?

3. How might you be tempted to glorify certain ministries while demeaning others?

What can you do to build unity within the body and, at the same time, give honor to the less visible but very important ministries?

4. What spiritual gifts has God given to you, and how are you using them to build up the body of Christ?

STUDY NINE

1 Corinthians 13:1-13

The Most Excellent Way

There are few words that have suffered more abuse in our society than the word *love*. Early in life we came to recognize the multifaceted meaning of "love." I can recall my mother, when I was quite young, explaining to me that you could love a person, but you could not love chocolate ice cream. And while I heard her rational explanation, and even accepted it to some extent, I still knew, down deep in my heart, that I *loved* chocolate ice cream.

And then there's the popularly accepted meaning of love today. Based on entertainment media definitions, love is totally glandular. There's love at first sight, falling in love, and making love. But in almost every case, love is presented as synonymous with sexual relationships. On this basis, love could be a one-night stand, living together, or simply recreational activity.

But the love of 1 Corinthians 13 is totally foreign to any of these definitions. "Love" in this chapter is the English translation of the Greek word *agape*. It is the kind of love that God manifests toward us—the kind of love that Christ showed when He came to live on the earth, and then to die for us. It is a giving, selfless, expecting-nothing-in-return kind of love.

Agape love is the love a parent expresses when that parent does what is inconvenient and difficult because it is best for the child. Agape love means determining what is best for another and then doing that because you love that person. Love that gives without any thought of return is the subject of this study.

First Corinthians 13 is the most beautiful and the most accurate ode to love ever written. Under the inspiration of the Holy Spirit, Paul may have written it before he penned this letter to the Corinthians. Or God's Spirit may have directed as Paul wrote the letter. Either way, it is a lyrical tribute to love—agape love as God defines it.

The Most Excellent Way

A. THE IMPORTANCE OF LOVE *(1 Cor. 13:1-3)*. Obviously, it is important what we do. Even with good motivation, doing the wrong thing still is wrong. But it is possible to do the right thing with the wrong attitude. And in God's eyes, it then becomes the wrong thing. In this first section we read about the importance of the right way.

Explaining the Text	*Examining the Text*
1. The Greek word here for love is *agape*, Godlike love, rather than *phileo*, which carries the connotation of brotherly love.	1. Read 1 Corinthians 13:1-3. Paul wrote describing the most excellent way in this chapter. What do you think is the less excellent way that he contrasted?
2. To the Greek mind, the eloquence of oratory was a prize to be valued highly. Some may have followed the skillful orator Apollos and scorned Paul because of his weak speech (3:4-7; cp. 2:1-3; 2 Cor. 10:1, 10).	2. What might be some qualities of an orator such as Paul mentioned? (v. 1)
3. "Resounding gong" can be the great noise that comes from any brass instrument—big and impressive, but fading almost immediately (similar to our expression "full of hot air").	3. What is the picture that Paul presented of an eloquent orator who is lacking in love? (v. 1)
	4. What are some of the qualities of prophecy and faith that Paul described? (v. 2)
	How could people with these gifts have an impact in the church?

Examining the Text	Explaining the Text
What are such gifts worth without selfless giving—without love? (v. 2)	
5. What two activities did Paul describe in verse 3? How could they influence the church? How valuable are they without love? (v. 3) 6. Write a brief paraphrase of verses 1-3.	5. Jesus vividly portrayed the contrast between a concern for the poor and expression of love when He was anointed in Bethany at the home of Simon the Leper (Mark 14:3-9). He did not condemn a concern for the poor but clarified that love also is critical.

B. THE QUALITIES OF LOVE *(1 Cor. 13:4-7)*. Most of us struggle with the meaning of abstract concepts. And so in order to clarify, Paul stated the actual qualities of a person who is operating on the love principle. He explained what such a person is and is not, what the person does and does not do.

Examining the Text	Explaining the Text
1. Read 1 Corinthians 13:4-7. Make two lists of how love is described. In the first list, write what love is or does. In the second, write what it is not or does not do. *Love Is/Does* *Love Is Not/Does Not*	1. In this section love is personified, which is a literary device where a thing or a concept is described as if it were a person—a living human being. Actually, this chapter describes how a Christian would act living a life characterized by agape love. But Paul described that person as if it were love doing these things.

The Most Excellent Way

Explaining the Text	Examining the Text
	2. Compare and contrast these with the fruit of the Spirit (Gal. 5:22-23) and the acts of the sinful nature (Gal. 5:17-21).
3. Since many of these qualities are contrary to our human nature, it is only God's Holy Spirit who is able to produce this type of selfless love consistently.	3. Try to identify people, both from the Bible and from those living today, who are good representatives of love.

C. THE ENDURANCE OF LOVE *(1 Cor. 13:8-13)*. Recently I heard someone described as "a whole lot better than his brother thinks he is, but not nearly as good as his mother believes." All of us are less than we could be, but the real question is whether or not we are growing. Are we moving from less to more mature?

Explaining the Text	Examining the Text
1. These three gifts seem to be foundational gifts; that is, particularly important for the establishing of the New Testament church. They were less needed after the church was well established.	1. Read 1 Corinthians 13:8-13. What three gifts will cease? (vv. 8-9) How are they contrasted with love? (v. 8)
2. "Perfection" and "imperfect" could better be translated "complete" and "incomplete."	2. How are these three gifts described? (vv. 9-10)
3. "Perfection" (that which is complete) has been the subject of great debate among Bible interpreters. Some feel it de-	3. What analogy did Paul use to describe the progress from imperfect to perfect? (v. 11)

Examining the Text

What happens to the imperfect? (v. 10)

4. How does the analogy of childhood relate both to the local church and also to individual believers?

5. What is our present perception of truth? (v. 12)

What can we expect in the future? (v. 12)

6. What three great doctrinal concepts did Paul end this chapter with? (v. 13)

Which of these is supremely important?

Explaining the Text

scribes the completion of the Bible; others, the maturity of the church; and still others think the return of Christ. Verse 12 seems to support this third option.

5. One of the ways that we can increase our understanding of the truth (which includes deeper knowledge of Christ) is through our study of the Bible, the truth of God.

Experiencing the Text

1. Briefly describe a church that has all of the gifts mentioned in this chapter, but that has little or no love being expressed.

Describe one where love is expressed.

Which of these is more like your church?

2. Do a brief self-inventory. What are the areas where you most exhibit the qualities of love?

Where could you use additional help and encouragement?

Take time to pray and ask God to assist and strengthen you in living a life that is characterized by agape love.

3. How would the practical application of this biblical love—selfless, giving, expecting-nothing-in-return love—change your relationships in:

Your home?

Your church?

Your workplace?

Your neighborhood?

STUDY TEN
1 Corinthians 14:1-40

Nurturing a Well-balanced Church

God has designed our bodies with a marvelous intricacy that defies imagination. Our body systems each are comprised of countless subsystems. And if one of these subsystems does not function properly, it affects the entire body. When we think about all of the potential systems that could malfunction within our bodies, it is a marvel that any of us is healthy any of the time.

Yet many of us do enjoy year after year of carefree health. We expect our bodies to function if we take care of them, and generally that is the case. If we get adequate rest, eat properly, and exercise regularly we usually live healthy lives.

But if we push too hard, we have problems. What if we stay up late and rise early in the morning? With insufficient sleep we soon become ill-tempered with bad judgment. The key to effective, healthy living is the proper amount of sleep.

Diet is another area that requires attention. We need to plan a balanced diet; otherwise our bodies will not function well. Of course, we can have too much of a good thing too, and then our bodies will begin to store excessive amounts of food as fat.

A similar principle applies to exercise. When we get the proper amount, our cardiovascular system will function at its peak of performance. Heart, lungs, veins, arteries, and many other parts will keep clicking along, healthy and happy. But improper exercise can excessively break down muscle and overstrain bones and connecting tissue.

We can experience maximum health only when all systems function in their proper balance. So also in the church. Spiritual gifts are important to effective functioning. Without them the body of Christ is unhealthy. But if any is taken to excess, it will weaken the church. We need gifts of ministry exercised, and we need them in proper proportions for the church to remain strong and healthy.

Nurturing a Well-balanced Church

A. THE GIFTS OF TONGUES AND PROPHECY *(1 Cor. 14:1-12).* Some of the Corinthians had become quite enamored with the excitement of the gift of tongues. And in so doing, they completely ignored the intent of spiritual gifts. The Corinthians had been using them to draw attention to themselves instead of building up the body.

Explaining the Text	*Examining the Text*
1. After the interlude of chapter 13, Paul resumed the theme of desiring the greater gifts—that is, those that edified the church.	1. Read 1 Corinthians 14:1-12. What twofold exhortation did Paul give to bring together the use of spiritual gifts and love? (v. 1) How should love influence the use of spiritual gifts? (v. 1)
2. In Acts 2:1-12, speaking in tongues definitely was speaking in a human language that the speaker did not know. Some feel that Corinthian tongues were the same. Others feel this was a heavenly language, not known to man.	2. Who was being addressed when a believer spoke in tongues? (v. 2)
	3. Which of the two (speaking in tongues or prophecy) did Paul say is a better gift? (vv. 2-6) Why is that a better one?
4. Ministering with the gift of prophecy had a double function. It included revealing new truth (since the Bible was not yet complete), and it also served to teach and instruct believers in God's Word.	4. How does prophecy reinforce Paul's basic teaching about the purpose of spiritual gifts? (vv. 3-5)

The First Epistle to the Corinthians

Examining the Text

5. What was Paul's intent when he came to the Corinthians? (v. 6)

6. What comparison did Paul make when he explained the importance of intelligible communication? (vv. 7-9)

7. What kinds of languages do you think that Paul was referring to here? (vv. 10-11)

Why do you think that God doesn't simply give this gift to all foreign missionaries?

Explaining the Text

6. The flute and harp were wind and string instruments used to entertain, while the trumpet was brass and often used to signal and inspire troops in military ventures.

7. Verses 10 and 11 seem to imply that these were earthly languages, known by someone, but not necessarily the one who was speaking.

B. THE LIMITATION OF SPEAKING IN TONGUES *(1 Cor. 14:13-20).* Christianity is not just one emotional high after another. Paul taught the importance of using our minds—our intellectual ability—with understanding as we worship and serve God.

Examining the Text

1. Read 1 Corinthians 14:13-20. What is the obvious limitation of speaking in tongues? (v. 14)

How could this problem be eliminated? (v. 13)

Explaining the Text

Nurturing a Well-balanced Church

Explaining the Text	*Examining the Text*
2. Paul distinguished between worshiping with the spirit and with the mind. While ecstatic utterances may have inspired the spirit, they did nothing to edify the mind.	2. What is a key objective in meeting together for group worship? (vv. 16-17) How can believers minister to each other, as well as direct their worship toward God? (v. 15)
3. "In the church" did not refer to a specific building, since there were no churches as such. It referred to an assembly of believers who met together for worship and other ministries.	3. What is the specific context in which Paul considered the value of speaking in tongues? (v. 19)
4. Paul obviously was not demeaning the gift of tongues, since he had used it repeatedly. From his own experience, he was addressing the importance of using it properly to edify the church, the body of Christ.	4. What was Paul's preference relative to speaking in tongues? (vv. 18-19) How does this clarify the importance of this particular gift? (v. 19)
5. Paul commended the innocence of children when it comes to understanding evil. Believers don't have to experience various forms of evil in order to be knowledgeable about it.	5. What did Paul want the Corinthians to stop doing? (v. 20) In what ways were their thoughts confused and their emphases inappropriate?

C. THE PURPOSE OF SPEAKING IN TONGUES *(1 Cor. 14:21-25).* Early in life most of us were taught the importance of using the right tool for the right purpose. While the Corinthians may have had a good tool—tongues—they were using it for the wrong purposes.

Examining the Text	*Explaining the Text*
1. Read 1 Corinthians 14:21-25. How had God prophesied that He would speak to his people (the Israelites)? (v. 21) But what would be their response? (v. 21)	1. Many evangelists who preached the Gospel in the first century were not Jews. Tongues in Acts 2:1-11 inaugurated the church, and later (Acts 8:9-13; 10:44-48) the gift of tongues demonstrated that non-Jews could be in the church too.
2. Who were the ones that benefited (other than the speaker) when someone spoke in an unknown tongue? (v. 22) What did the believers need? (v. 22)	2. According to the context, the unbelievers probably were skeptical Jews. Speaking in tongues was to authenticate the basic Gospel message. Prophecy would have been giving new revelation and teaching God's Word.
3. What gift really is significant to the life and the growth of the church? (vv. 23-25)	
4. How would a newcomer react to speaking in tongues in the assembly of believers? (v. 23) How would a newcomer react to prophecy (the giving and teaching of God's Word)? (vv. 24-25)	4. Paul's emphasis was that tongues indicated God was doing a new work, perhaps as the Gospel went into a new area. After a church had been established, deeper instruction in the Word was needed to help those believers mature.

D. GUIDELINES FOR MINISTERING THROUGH SPIRITUAL GIFTS *(1 Cor. 14:26-40).* It's usually easier to put something together when you follow the directions. Paul gave the directions for the use of spiritual gifts so that Christians might contribute to the growth of the church.

Nurturing a Well-balanced Church

Explaining the Text

1. "Brothers" was a term that Paul used to refer to fellow Christians, both male and female.

2. Obviously, speaking in tongues was something over which the individual had control. He could decide whether to speak or not.

5. Paul did not forbid women to participate (cp. 11:5, 13). Some feel that due to the religious prostitutes in pagan Corinth, Christian women had to be

Examining the Text

1. Read 1 Corinthians 14:26-40. What are some ways in which Christians could have contributed to corporate worship in Corinth? (v. 26)

What general guideline was to be followed? (v. 26)

2. What four guidelines were to govern speaking in tongues if they were to be used in the assembly of believers? (vv. 27-28)

3. What basic regulations controlled use of the gift of prophecy in the church? (vv. 29-31)

What was the result of allowing the appropriate use of this gift? (v. 31)

4. What did Paul teach should be the general tenor of a worship service? (v. 33)

How could control be exercised? (v. 32)

5. How were women to secure answers to questions that they may have had? (v. 35)

Examining the Text

What was to be their demeanor in the worship service? (v. 34)

6. What restrictions did Paul express regarding the use of any spiritual gifts? (vv. 37-39)

7. What should be a believer's attitude toward using spiritual gifts? (v. 39)

According to verse 40, what should be the procedure to follow?

Explaining the Text

especially careful. Others feel that perhaps women, seated apart from their husbands, were calling out to them seeking answers.

6. Apparently, Paul felt that the credibility of anyone exercising spiritual gifts corresponded with that person's willingness to follow the guidelines from God.

Experiencing the Text

1. What are some of the less glamorous positions in your church that are hard to staff?

How could a better understanding of the place and purpose of spiritual gifts help to alleviate such staffing problems?

2. In what ways have you observed self-centered or childish behavior by people who have local-church ministry responsibility?

Nurturing a Well-balanced Church

What does this tell you about their understanding of spiritual gifts and the nature of their ministry?

3. What role does God's Word play in your life, and how could it become a more vital influence in all that you do and say?

4. What changes in your local church could enable it to minister more effectively?

What could you do personally to improve the quality of your church's ministry?

STUDY ELEVEN

1 Corinthians 15:1-34

Believers Assured of Resurrection

Sometimes it is very difficult to know whom we should believe. Virtually every product manufacturer assures the consumer that its products are totally dependable. "We'll stake our reputation on our quality." But in some cases neither reputation nor quality are worth very much.

Occasionally even a manufacturer with an excellent reputation can prove to be less than satisfactory. Presently we are struggling with an ailing central vacuum cleaning unit in our house. When our house was being built we realized that we could install a central unit for about the same cost as a good vacuum cleaner. Since it was going to last for the life of the house, we chose the unit carefully, selecting a system from a major manufacturer known for availability of parts and service.

What we didn't count on was the decision of that company to discontinue selling central vacuum units. Now, ten years later, we find that it is impossible to get the exact parts that are needed for repair. And so we are adapting and modifying similar parts to keep the unit working.

As you can well imagine, I am leery of making other major purchases from this particular company. My confidence is no better than my most recent experience. And when a company has failed to make good on its commitment, it is very hard to get excited about future expectations.

Some of the Corinthians were questioning the future. They contradicted Paul, and indicated that really there would be no resurrection of those who died—that Paul was wrong in his teaching. But Paul's reply demolished their speculative assertions. Since Jesus rose from the dead, we each can look forward to a similar experience. In fact, Jesus was only the first of many. And we can be assured that just as He rose from the dead, we too can anticipate resurrection. We can trust His reputation.

Believers Assured of Resurrection

A. THE GOSPEL PAUL PREACHED *(1 Cor. 15:1-11)*. Some people claim that Christians alone operate on the basis of faith. But we are not the only ones who believe in something. Everyone believes in something. The really important question is, "What is the object of your faith?" Paul clearly presented the content of the Christian's faith—what it is that we believe.

Explaining the Text	*Examining the Text*
1. The word *gospel* is a compound word in which the word for good is united with the word for message or news. The Gospel is the "Good News."	1. Read 1 Corinthians 15:1-11. What were the three steps in the Corinthians receiving the message of the Gospel from Paul? (v. 1)
	2. According to verse 2, what was the important thing for the Corinthians to do with the Good News that they had received?
3. One of the very important questions that the early church faced was, "What, exactly, is the Gospel message on which we are basing our entire hope?" These verses contain one of the earliest creeds (statements of belief) of the early church.	3. List the essential elements of the Gospel as Paul described them in verses 3-5. Why is it very important for all believers to be totally clear on these elements of the Gospel?
4. It is significant that when Paul wrote about the resurrection of Christ, many of those whom he mentioned still were alive, and these could have contradicted his statements if they were false.	4. What was the sequence of Christ's appearing to people following the Resurrection? (vv. 5-8) Why is it important that He appeared to different people, in different contexts, over some extended period of time?

Examining the Text	Explaining the Text
5. Why did Paul feel as though he was the least deserving to be an apostle? (v. 9)	5. Paul was not one of the first 12 Apostles, but later was chosen specifically by Christ after His ascension to heaven (Acts 9:1-9).
6. What enabled Paul to become an apostle? (v. 10) And how did he approach serving after becoming one? (vv. 10-11)	

B. THE MEANING OF JESUS' RESURRECTION *(1 Cor. 15:12-19)*.

Sometimes the best way to refute an argument is to show the logical extension of accepting that point of view. In this section, Paul demonstrated what conclusions Christians would have to accept if we were to believe those who maintained that there is no such thing as bodily resurrection.

Examining the Text	Explaining the Text
1. Read 1 Corinthians 15:12-19. What was the incompatibility between what some were claiming about resurrection and what Paul taught? (v. 12)	1. This section is a hypothetical argument to raise the questions that would have to be answered if one assumed (incorrectly) that those who died could not be raised.
2. What would be the inevitable conclusion if the dead were not to be raised? (v. 13) And how would that conclusion affect the Gospel message and those who had believed in it? (v. 14)	2. The Sadducees (wealthy Jewish leaders) did not believe in the resurrection. Apparently some of the Christians in the early church were guilty of the same error, and were proclaiming it in Corinth.

Believers Assured of Resurrection

Explaining the Text	*Examining the Text*
	3. What would have happened to the credibility of those eyewitnesses who claimed to have viewed Christ after His resurrection? (v. 15)
4. If any one part of the message of the Gospel were found to be false, then doubt would be cast on the entire message. People could conclude that none of it is trustworthy.	4. If there were no such thing as bodily resurrection, then what would we have to accept about Jesus' being raised from the dead? (v. 16) And what would be the implication for faith in the Gospel? (v. 17) 5. In verses 17-18, how is the fact of the Resurrection of Christ tied inextricably to the message of the Gospel? (cp. v. 4)
6. Obviously, blind, unfounded faith was considered by Paul to have absolutely no value at all. He was interested in a faith built on unshakable fact.	6. If Jesus had not been raised from the dead bodily (assuming that there were no Resurrection), what hope would believers have for the future beyond this life? (v. 19)

C. THE EXPECTATION OF BELIEVERS' RESURRECTION *(1 Cor. 15:20-34).* When we really believe something, it should be evident through the way that we live. Paul pleaded for consistency and just such demonstration in the lives of Christians.

Explaining the Text	*Examining the Text*
1. Firstfruits were the choice early pickings, before the full crop matured. The first ripe fruit was a promise of the bountiful harvest to come.	1. Read 1 Corinthians 15:20-34. On what factual basis did Paul build the preaching of the Gospel? (v. 20)

Examining the Text	Explaining the Text
2. Name the two men through whom life and death entered the human race (vv. 21-22).	
What are some similarities and dissimilarities between these two?	
3. In what way was Jesus Christ a firstfruit? (v. 23)	3. Jesus sometimes is referred to as the Second Adam. Just as Adam was the first of the human race, so also Jesus was the first of new humanity—those who would be born-again spiritually to new life.
And in what way was Adam?	
4. What must Christ do before He ushers in the new kingdom that will last for all eternity? (vv. 24-27)	4. Jesus could operate with the full authority of God since He also is a member of the Godhead.
What is the one exception to the "all things" that have been subjected to Christ? (v. 27)	
5. What is the relationship between God and Christ? (v. 28)	5. While members of the Godhead (Father, Son, and Holy Spirit) have different functions and responsibilities, all are totally equal.
6. What kinds of things did people do that demonstrated they really believed that the dead would be resurrected eventually? (vv. 29-32)	6. Apparently, some who claimed that there would be no resurrection had been baptized on behalf of those who had died. Paul did not commend this practice; he merely showed the absurdity of their actions if

Believers Assured of Resurrection

Explaining the Text	*Examining the Text*
they did not believe in resurrection. They really must have felt there would be a resurrection.	What difference does it make in your life that we can anticipate living eternally with Christ after the resurrection? 7. How can believers protect against being misled into doctrinal error? (vv. 33-34)

Experiencing the Text

1. How might the fact of Paul's starting out by persecuting the church potentially have kept him from effective ministry to the church?

What experiences in your own life could have proven to be a hindrance to your service?

How does the grace of God free you from any such possible limitations?

2. Have you personally believed the message of the Gospel and accepted God's offer of eternal life? If not, why not pause right now and pray to God, telling Him that you believe the Gospel and want eternal life?

What difference does it make for you that Jesus was raised from the dead and that you can anticipate resurrection also?

3. In what ways do you act differently from non-Christians because you have been reborn spiritually and anticipate eternity in heaven with Christ?

STUDY TWELVE

1 Corinthians 15:35–16:24

Christians in the Future and the Present

Quite a few years ago, when our two younger sons were still preschoolers, we had an interesting conversation about heaven. Nathan, who was about four, and Kevin, who was six, had awakened before Elaine and me. As we were waking up, we heard Nathan and Kevin talking together quietly in Kevin's room.

"What's heaven going to be like?" asked Nathan. I held my breath straining to hear Kevin's answer. "Well, I don't know," replied Kevin in a rather glum voice, "but I think we're going to pray a lot."

It was obvious to me that Kevin and Nathan were far from looking forward to getting to heaven. Elaine and I felt that it was time for a little theological instruction. So I went into Kevin's room to discuss the topic of heaven with them. Since I never had a course in seminary that addressed the topic of teaching young children about heaven, I was searching for a way to describe it.

I sat down on the side of the bed and explained that Mom and I had heard them talking about heaven and thought maybe I could be of some help. I reminded them that earlier in the year we had spent some time together as a family in Florida. One of the places that we had visited was Disney World. Naturally they remembered the good time that we had on our trip. I explained to them that I really didn't know what heaven was going to be like exactly. But I did know one thing for sure. I knew that whatever they thought about Disney World, heaven was going to be better than that.

Paul knew that the Corinthians also were confused about heaven. And some were even wondering if there was anything to look forward to. He closed this letter to the church at Corinth by helping to change their understanding of the future. We don't know for sure what heaven will be like, but we all should be looking forward to eternity there.

Christians in the Future and the Present

A. THE NATURE OF RESURRECTED BODIES *(1 Cor. 15:35-49)*. It's always difficult to explain something to someone when what you are trying to explain is totally beyond their experience. In order to explain about the nature of resurrection, Paul resorted to the use of analogies, showing how some things with much in common still differ.

Explaining the Text	*Examining the Text*
1. Verses 36-38 answer the first question, and verses 39-41 answer the second one.	1. Read 1 Corinthians 15:35-49. What two questions did Paul seek to answer in this section? (v. 35)
2. Although seeds give the appearance of death when they are buried in the ground out of sight, actually planting (burial) is necessary in order for the new life to emerge from the seed.	2. What earthly metaphor (comparison) did Paul use to describe the relationship between our present bodily life and our resurrected life? (vv. 36-38) What are some of the elements that make this a particularly appropriate comparison?
3. Paul selected several categories of created things, and he showed how the things in each category differ in spite of having much in common.	3. What are the categories of created things that Paul chose as an example? (vv. 39-41)
4. In these verses, Paul explained that although our earthly bodies and resurrected bodies have much in common, they also have significant differences.	4. What are the differences between our earthly bodies and our resurrected bodies? (vv. 42-44) *Earthly* *Resurrected*

Examining the Text	*Explaining the Text*
5. According to verses 45-49, what are the differences between Adam (and his descendants) and Christ (and His descendants)?	5. Just as Adam was the first man in the human race, Jesus is the first of a new race—those who will experience eternal life through Christ's death on the cross (cp. Rom. 5:12-19).

B. ANTICIPATION OF CHRIST'S RETURN *(1 Cor. 15:50-58)*. All of us wonder about the future. What will it be like? What will happen to us? Paul provided some answers to these and other questions in this passage.

Examining the Text	*Explaining the Text*
1. Read 1 Corinthians 15:50-58. According to verse 50, what would keep us from dwelling in the kingdom of God right now?	1. While the term "kingdom of God" may have various connotations, it usually refers to God's reign; and here it refers to heaven.
2. What changes will enable us to inhabit God's kingdom? (vv. 51-54)	
3. How will the change from mortal to immortal occur? (v. 52) How will this instantaneous transformation fulfill the prophecy in Hosea 13:14? (vv. 54-55)	3. Those who believe that Christians will remain on earth for all or part of the Tribulation would relate this to one of the trumpets in Revelation (perhaps the seventh, Rev. 11:15). Those who feel the church will not remain for the Tribulation would see this as the Rapture of the church (1 Thes. 4:13-18).

Christians in the Future and the Present

Explaining the Text	*Examining the Text*
4. The law of God depicts the absolute standards of God that all of us fail to measure up to.	4. What is the consequence of our failure to fully obey the law of God in all aspects? (v. 56)
	5. According to verse 57, what is the reason that we all can praise God?
6. "Therefore" is a very strong expression that is used to present a concluding statement, probably tying up all of the challenges in this letter.	6. What two challenges did Paul give to Christians in light of our anticipation of eternity? (v. 58)
	7. Why should we give ourselves fully to the work of serving the Lord? (v. 58)

C. SPIRITUAL GENEROSITY *(1 Cor. 16:1-4)*. It is normal and expected for Christians to provide financially to help other believers in need. But it always should be done in the proper manner. Paul explained how such giving could be done.

Explaining the Text	*Examining the Text*
1. This answer may refer back to one of the questions that the Corinthians had asked (1 Cor. 7:1).	1. Read 1 Corinthians 16:1-4. What was the purpose of collecting the money? (v. 1)
	Who else received similar instructions?

Examining the Text	*Explaining the Text*
2. List the specific guidelines given by Paul for providing money for others in need (v. 2).	2. Paul suggested a way to minister financially to the needs of other Christians without scurrying around frantically to collect money at the last minute.
3. Which believers in need did Paul intend the money to be sent to? (v. 3)	
How did Paul intend to get the gifts to the believers?	
4. What was Paul himself considering doing in association with the gift? (v. 4)	

D. CONCLUSIONS AND FINAL GREETINGS *(1 Cor. 16:5-24).* Since he had spent almost eighteen months helping to establish the church in Corinth, Paul found it very difficult to close this letter. Not only did he give final exhortations, but he shared many warm comments too.

Examining the Text	*Explaining the Text*
1. Read 1 Corinthians 16:5-24. What were some of the options that Paul was considering? (vv. 5-9)	
What was his motivating drive in relation to the Corinthians? (v. 7)	

Christians in the Future and the Present

Explaining the Text	*Examining the Text*
2. As Paul traveled on his missionary trips, he took men with him whom he trained, and also met some along the way. Timothy and Apollos were two whom he discipled.	2. What did Paul want to happen in regard to Timothy? (vv. 10-11)
	3. What did Paul expect from Apollos? (v. 12)
	4. What challenge (in the form of closing exhortations) did Paul give to the Corinthians? (vv. 13-14)
	How does this challenge summarize the Book of 1 Corinthians?
5. Even as Paul did not hesitate to confront those who sinned (cp. 5:1ff), he also commended those who did well.	5. How were Stephanas, Fortunatas, and Achaicus good models for the believers? (vv. 15-18)
	6. How do Paul's concluding comments help us to see the passion and drive of his life? (vv. 21-24)

Experiencing the Text

1. In what ways do we, as believers, demonstrate the qualities and characteristics of Adam through whom we received life?

And in what ways can we demonstrate the qualities and characteristics of the Second Adam through whom we received new life?

2. How does the anticipation of eternity with Christ motivate you to stand firm and give yourself to the work of the Lord?

3. In what ways are you able to help meet the financial needs of others?

What more could you do, or should you do?

4. Whom do you know that ought to be commended or thanked for faithfulness in service?

Why not decide to contact that person and express how you feel?

5. In what ways has your view of the Christian life changed through your study of 1 Corinthians?

What are you going to do differently because of this study?